IN MY WILDEST DREAMS TAKE 1

Wayne L Jackson #1

The Mar-Keys, 1961
Left to Right-*Wayne Jackson, Packy Axton, Steve Cropper, Don Nix, Ronnie "Angel" Stoots, Terry Johnson, Duck Dunn*

WAYNE JACKSON

Jackson and Jackson Publishing, Memphis, Tennessee

Credits

In My Wildest Dreams, Take I

Author

Wayne Jackson

Editor

Amy Jackson

Graphic Design and Production

Ronnie Stoots

Published in the United States by Wayne and Amy Jackson,
Memphis, Tennessee.

Unless otherwise noted, all photographs belong to The Wayne Jackson Collection.

Table Of Contents

Avon Calling 1

Across The River to Memphis 21

Here Come The Mar-Keys 52

Up In Smoke 67

Memphis Rocked 77

College at McLemore 86

Atlantic Crossing 102

Kings of The Road 125

The Summer of Love 133

The Hit Factories 142

A Change Is Gonna Come 154

Goodbye 163

Bonus Section

On The Record With Wayne 169

Discography 178

Foreword

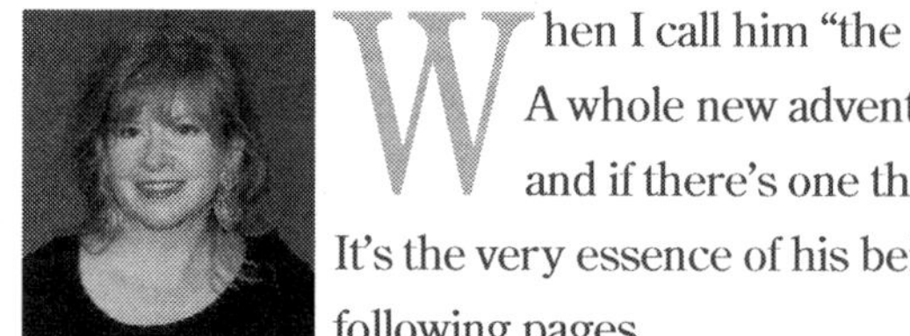

When I call him "the author," his green eyes twinkle. A whole new adventure is unfolding for Wayne, and if there's one thing he loves...it's an adventure. It's the very essence of his being, as you will see in the following pages.

Our adventure together began on March 28th, 1990, when Wayne walked through the doors of "The Evening Times," his hometown newspaper, for an interview with yours truly, the lifestyle editor. Exactly one week prior to this event, a psychic had told me "the one" was coming to me, my soul mate. Boy, did he hit the nail on the head!

Wayne asked me out to dinner the next night, and we've been together ever since.

From that very first meeting, I have been enthralled with the stories of Wayne's magical journey. The amazing thing is he's been writing them down in one form or another over the past five decades. While sorting through boxes of memorabilia, we found notebooks from 1966 describing the Mar-Keys' adventures, old journals from the Seventies and letters from the road to the folks back home. He'd already been writing short stories since the Eighties with the idea of a book always in the back of his mind, and by 1997, he had written enough for a top literary agent to pitch for a publishing deal. But for seven years, the publishers said there wasn't enough dirt on rock stars. And our thoughts began to turn to other projects.

We had been doing really well selling some memorabilia and found ourselves connecting with music lovers all over the world. And one day divine inspiration struck. Wayne walked into our office and said he thought we should put the book together ourselves and sell it. Forget the publishers, take it directly to the people!

As I heard him speak the words, I knew it was the right thing to do.

And so we began on possibly the biggest adventure of all in our twenty-one years of marriage...the birthing of this book.

Now, as we sit here today and look at the finished product, I believe Wayne's goal has been accomplished...you have in your hand an "All Access" pass to the backstage of music history...Take One.

A Note To The Reader

This book is not a historical document, nor is it a work of fiction. It is quite simply a book of my memories as I perceived them from my position at the head of my table, the one where my memories are scattered about. I apologize in advance for any distortions you may find concerning your possible memories of these events. I've done the best I can.

My great thanks to my friend, *Rob Bowman*, for kindly allowing me to keep his excellent book, "Soulsville U.S.A.," by my side as an occasional reference for time and place. It is an outstanding work.

And an even greater, loving thanks to my wife, *Amy Tenent Jackson*, without whose editorial talents and constant leadership this book would have never come into your hands in the light of day.

I'd also like to thank the following people who were magically there from the beginning leading me along the way:

Mrs. McCarley, who sparked my love of storytelling with her felt board and Bible character cutouts in elementary school; my parents, *Edna Mai* and *Giffin Jackson*, who gave me my first trumpet; *Doyne Dodd, Sr.*, who taught me how fun music is; *Phil Vance*, who taught me how to breath and play; *Ben White*, *Craig Tennison*, *Dick Zerby* and *Al Paudert*, who fostered my love of flying; *Wayne Walker*, who showed me what courage was all about; *Ronnie Stoots* and *Terry Johnson*, who asked me to join The Mar-Keys; *Estelle Axton*, who believed and opened the door; *Chips Moman*, who gave me my first hit record; *Robert Talley*, who taught me to solo; *Steve Cropper*, who asked me to come work at Stax; *Gene "Bowlegs" Miller* and *Floyd Newman*, my friends and mentors; *Andrew Love*, my best friend and business partner; *Jerry Wexler*, godfather of Rhythm and Blues, who took me to a level I never imagined; all the *friends* and *fans* who bought records and concert tickets supporting me in my chosen profession; and I thank *God* for creating the magic that still persists to this day.

I found deep satisfaction in pursuing this work, and I sincerely hope that you enjoy what I have written.

Wayne

Avon Calling

At home in Memphis in our beautiful Tudor cottage, standing in the red-tiled kitchen, thinking about nothing but what I'd cook for my lovely wife's dinner when she got home from the law office, I was startled when the phone rang.

A voice said, "Hello, this is Billy Frances with Sting's management. Is Wayne Jackson there?"

"Yes," I said, "this is he."

Sting? I thought.

"Sting wanted me to call and inquire if there is any interest between you and your partner in the Memphis Horns, Andrew Love, I think, for doing his upcoming album? We'd be recording sometime in late October over here at the Lake House."

Like I'd know where that was. "In England?"

"Yes," he replied coolly. "Salisbury, Wiltshire. Sting's home on the Salisbury Plain. It's called the Lake House."

I took the big step over to my half-barrel chair and sat down in it! I knew what was on the Salisbury Plain, all right! Stonehenge, the ancient and mysterious Druid holy site known to be at least five-thousand-years-old. A place I'd always wanted to visit, but somehow in my traveling around England had not gotten to.

"Well, yes! We're interested, for sure."

"Oh, good. Sting will be pleased to hear. Let me get some information from you, and we'll continue. How much money will you require to come to England and record for, let's say a week?"

I hate this part. I'm always afraid I won't ask for enough, they'll agree and I'll know I left a bundle on the table. Or I'll shoot too high, and they'll politely say, "all right, we'll get back to you," and never call again. Especially the British. So nice and always in control. My mind went cloudy like it gets when confronted with "the big time." I said, "We're used to getting fifteen hundred dollars each, per recording day." I wanted this gig but had no idea what other players of our stature could expect and never have. We hadn't had management since the Seventies. There really wasn't enough commission involved in recording sessions to get a good one interested, although we had tried.

"Plus everything else and per-diem," I concluded. Everything else being plane fare, hotels and meals, tips included. I felt miserable but elated at the same time. STING! A tour with him would surely pull us from the doldrums.

"Got that," Billy said. "Per-diem is usually fifty per day. That okay?"

"Sure," I said.

That's more than others, I thought. And there I was, back fighting small time thinking. Again!

"We're on then," he said. "You'll be getting paper work from a bunch called Grubman Indursky Shindler & Goldstein, P.C., in London and Sting's manager in L.A., Mr. Miles Copeland. Don't let any of them scare you, they're just doing what they have to do!"

He laughed a friendly and sincere laugh like road managers are obliged to laugh during times of stress. A comforting noise to any musician in the face of the unknown. I was used to guys like this taking care of me and felt safer with his instant familiarity. They are a musician's anchor to reality and know everything you don't. I was "in his charge" from then on, and I felt I had a friend in Billy.

Amy was excited about the possibility of a tour, also, except for the time apart. We agreed to wait and see, though. First, the recording.

Correspondence began arriving in early September, and there was a steady bunch of thick, manila envelopes in our mailbox almost daily. They were massive documents, and it took a lot of time just reading them. We would deal with each one individually, sign properly, return and wait for more.

There was a lot of information needed for our work permits in the U.K., something we were familiar with at least. All this was handled by Davenport Lyons of London. Our mailman, Bob, gained huge respect for Amy and I during this time. One hot day, I offered him a cold drink, and he took me up on it. I think just to check out the inside of our house. He wasn't disappointed. Gold and platinum albums lined the stairwell from bottom to top, and trophies and plaques filled the entertainment center. You know, music's what I do for a living, and I'm proud of my accomplishments. We were friends from then on.

Then one day a fax arrived from Miles Copeland at First Star in L.A. He wanted to haggle with us over the price of recording with Sting. He wanted us to go for one thousand per day, instead of the fifteen hundred I had agreed to. Everything else was the same. I was shocked that this small amount would matter to a big-time rock and roll star.

But this was Miles, Sting's manager. He must have been trying to get a point across of some kind. It tickled at the back of my mind. That little voice was straining to be heard, but I closed it out and sat down with the fax to brood. This jerk hadn't even signed it. So no real proof he'd ever sent it! Arrogance came to mind, but I realized I had some of that also and didn't want to blow this opportunity to hook up with a big star again, make money and have a good time. Ego comes into play and self-preservation, too. Luckily. Easy boy, don't let him get that quick goat of yours! You know how much trouble that's caused in the past.

When Amy came home, we discussed this and decided the only thing to do was go along with this Miles guy and get to England where we would be a big hit with Sting himself, and then we'd be in the driver's seat. Yes, that would be our approach to this bump in the road.

So I sent a fax back agreeing to Miles' terms. Everything was groovy again.

November came to Memphis, and our trees went crimson, yellow, orange and tawny brown. Their leaves fell to earth by the ton. It's a time when the breeze has a little bite in it, and warm sweaters by the hearth feel good.

Hearts were light and filled with thoughts of the coming Christmas, so when the two, strong-looking, young men in the old Pontiac pulled up in our drive and offered to clean up the yard for eighty bucks, we held our arms open wide and sang out, "Sure!"

When they left, there was a mountain of green leaf bags sitting out in the street.

Later, at two-thirty a.m., the burglar alarm went off, and while stumblin' and stumpin' my toes in the dark, I managed to find my gun. I went to the windows to look out but could see nothing unusual and knew I'd have to venture outside if I wanted to find the breach in our security and perhaps the villains who perpetrated the deed. God, I was shaken.

I went to the back door and peered out into the night now bright from the emergency lights. Nobody there.

I eased out the door and went down the driveway to the gate I'd carefully closed earlier. A stockade-style, wooden affair with a little, drop-latch. I stood on tiptoes to get a look over. No beat up car. Nothing. I'd have to actually push the gate open if I wanted to investigate further. I did, and there in the shadows of the portico was our basement door, standing open just two inches, exposing the blackness inside.

Did I mention it was VERY cold? That's why my knees were knocking, and my hands couldn't hold the flashlight steady nor the rifle.

I made as much racket as possible, clearing my throat and scraping my feet on the blacktop. Then I just shined the light into the blackness and pushed the door all the way open. Nothing there. Not even the leaf-blowing machine! DAMN!

The same guys I'd paid eighty bucks to that afternoon to clean us out had come back to finish us off. We later noticed our bicycles were missing, too.

The police called and said they'd come by the next day to take a report. The burglar alarm folks called, and Amy told them we had it under control.

All except that part where I would be away for a week to go to the king's castle, leaving Amy home alone!

The giant Northwest Airline 747 sat on the west end of runway nine, and the four Pratt & Whitney engines howled their distress at having to leave the earth. Nonetheless, they hurled hurricane force hot gases backwards until the plane began its lumbering gait towards one hundred eighty knots at the other end of the runway. Once there, she lifted her dainty nose skyward and stepped lightly off into the cool, blue November afternoon. With that she climbed to a respectable altitude just before adjusting her course slightly to the northeast for the trip up the eastern seaboard, then out across the night sea towards Holland.

When the flight attendant came around offering drinks, Andrew and I gladly accepted two, small bottles of water each. We'd long ago learned the perils of alcohol and long flights. We had meals, watched movies and slept on and off until the early morning hours, when we arrived in Amsterdam. We suffered through the usual immigration stuff and in time boarded a British Airways flight to London's Heathrow Airport. It took about an hour, and after landing and repeating the immigration process, we found ourselves at the passenger pick-up port with our bags and horns, looking for our driver. Our difference in color must be a dead giveaway, because shortly, a man walked over to us with a cardboard sign that read, "Memphis Horns," and took us over to a beautiful, black Jaguar sedan to load us in. I asked how long a drive it was to "the house," and he replied, "Oh, about two and a half I should think, if there's no trouble on the road."

We both got in the back seat thinking of a nap, but that rarely works for me in foreign countries. I need to SEE everything!

I began a dialogue with the driver and made him talk the whole time we were driving through the wonderful English countryside, in the car of my dreams. I learned a lot about Wiltshire. Andrew listened for a bit and dozed off from time to time. He's lucky that way.

The Lake House sat beside the Avon River on forty acres of absolutely, lush gardens. The house itself was three stories of checkered stone with windows all around and at least ten chimneys atop the red-tiled roof. It had five, triangular peaks across the front and the same in back with figures at the summit of each. It's a fifteenth century castle after all and quite impressive.

The front door was wooden and massive, encased in a huge, granite archway with five-tiered steps of stone leading down to the orange pea gravel driveway we arrived on.

No sooner than our car stopped rolling, a man dressed impeccably in black trousers and shoes and a stiffly, starched, white shirt with bow tie came smoothly down the steps, hand already extended to welcome us.

"Oh, GOOD, GOOD!" he exclaimed. "You must be Mr. Jackson," he said, giving my hand a strong pump, "and you're Mr. Love!" Andrew got a pump, too. "We're so glad you've arrived safe and sound! I'll get you into your rooms, and then Sting will be down to greet you. He's SO excited and can't wait to show you around!"

It turned out his name was John, and he was the butler and boss of the house. No doubt about that either. Second only to Sting in the chain of command.

The driver opened the boot, as the British say, and began getting our bags out and carrying them up the stairs and into the house. We followed and entered what can only be thought of as a movie set of old England. A three-story entry hall with a three landing staircase going up the far wall to other floors, including the second one where our rooms were located.

We had just enough time to go to the bathroom and wash the flight film off our faces and hands before meeting back up in the hall and walking to the door that led back to the stairwell.

I don't know if Sting plans these things for effect or not, but the effect was enough to make me a little nervous. I couldn't tell about Andrew and never can. He's smooth and cool at all times, unless he's on an airplane that's being tossed around the sky.

We opened the door and stepped out onto the landing to begin our descent. I couldn't help but reflect on the castles we had visited in the Seventies while making records with Rod Stewart and Stephen Stills and how different each one felt.

Suddenly, a voice of slightly nasal quality boomed out from below, "WELL! THE MEMPHIS HORNS! I've been waiting for this moment a long time! Welcome."

And there, standing on the stone floor of the entryway, was the king. Sting.

His jackboots were of a dark color and well used. They went up to three inches below his knee. He wore tan riding breaches with a tawny shirt tucked in, no belt and a day coat of wool that was open in the front and hung just below the knees.

We shook hands and said hellos.

"How was your flight?"

"Oh, fine," I answered, "a little long, as usual, but we're doin' good!" Andrew said something to the same effect.

"Excellent! Come on, now, and I'll show you around the place we call Lake House." We went down a few steps into a large turret that served as a library and then down two more into the kitchen where John was over-seeing the preparation of the evening meal. From there, it was only a few steps through a screen door to the outdoors. Sting picked up a twisted, wooden walking stick, which he carried on his right side. He was in a very good mood as we started our trek about the property.

"You'll see boys, we've made Lake House like a little fort. We can maintain independently from the outside world if we have to." We were walking down towards a boathouse sitting on pylons in the river. It had large windows on every side, so the river views from inside were perfect.

"This is where I often come to think and write. It's very serene here. And there is the generator for the power to the property underneath. The Avon River has enough volume to support us through the generator all year round."

He seemed very proud of it. We were properly impressed and said so.

Then we turned and walked off farther from the house. It was getting cooler now, and I wished I had brought my own sweater. We came to a big, glassed-in area that was the hot house. "We grow our own vegetables and flowers here. All year long."

"Kind of like Jules Verne on dry land?" I joked.

He laughed and said, "Yes, that's it!"

"We have dairy animals and sheep elsewhere on the land."

The grass was thick and lush under my sneakers. The air felt crisp on my cheek, and it smelled of greenery and wood smoke from the house fires. Everywhere the shrubs and flowering bushes were perfectly trimmed.

Thatched-roof cottages encircled the main house, and although I basically knew what they were, I asked anyway. "What are those little houses around the grounds?"

"Those are servant quarters. Long ago, the people who worked on the place lived here as well. It was part of their arrangement. The cobbler might live in that one there, and the seamstress over there. The cook there. The butler would be in this one here and so on. It was very convenient when there were no trains or buses to a nearby town. We're putting them back in livable condition for our workers now."

You could see they were works in progress.

The sun was dipping lower, right along with the temperatures. I was so cold and tired I could hardly speak. At least we were headed back towards the house and that beckoning fireplace.

We walked into the entryway with our arms folded, stomping our feet. I'm sure my nose was red and running like when I hunted rabbit as a kid in Arkansas during the winter.

I felt like one of the band now. Initiated by the long trek!

"Well," said Sting, "when would you boys like to begin work?" His eyes were fairly twinkling.

It was around four p.m., and we'd been going a long time with no rest. I said, "We'd like a little time to shower and change and maybe lie down for an hour if that would be okay with you?"

His face didn't reflect pleasure. It was obvious he wanted to start right away. "Well," he said, with the slightest frown, "dinner is half six, so take until five-thirty and get a little rest. We'll have an hour or so to go over the first song and throw some ideas around. How's that suit? All right?"

Any sort of rest suited us just fine. We both nodded and said we'd be down at five-thirty ready to go. At last, he smiled back at us and said, "Off you go then. Until later."

And off we went, dragging our asses up the stairs and onto the second floor.

My room was rather small compared to modern, luxury hotels, but this was, after all, a castle. There was a small dresser with hanging mirror, a chair that did look medieval and a bunk bed. My small bag (I travel light) was on the top bunk, and I pulled it down and got out clean underwear, socks and shaving gear and lay back on the lower bunk for a moment. Whew! My bones were aching from all the sitting on the plane, and my feet were still cold from the walk. That hot shower was going to be just what the doctor ordered! Maybe it would wash away some of the fog from the jet lag and get me all right for who knew what was coming this evening.

The bathroom, two doors down from me, was definitely not ancient. All polished tiles and gleaming Swedish chrome and porcelain. It was so beautiful and European, it made me smile. I eyed the hanging showerhead on the long, snaking, silver hose and almost groaned with anticipated pleasure. I decided on the shower first and then a shave.

The bathtub was soaking size, but I knew I didn't have time for that, maybe later. The spigot heads were bigger than my hand and resembled ship's steering wheels. I put my hands on them and gave them a big spin together for maximum effect and nothing much happened. Just a dribble from the faucet. Drip, drip, drip. Gurgle, drip, drip. Finally, the dribbling and gurgling got warmer.

It was then that I noticed the black, plastic bucket and stool sitting by the tub. My heart sank. OH, NO! No water pressure on the king's second floor! I was standing there naked, a little cool and shaken. I went over to the window and cranked it out. Sure enough, there were the cottages and immaculate grounds and perfectly trimmed drive. But NO hot shower for me! I took down some fine, thick, white towels from the warming rack and laid them in the floor to protect my feet from frostbite and wanted to cry.

Oh well. When in England!

So I put the black bucket under the faucet and let the dripping water start to slowly fill it while I sat on the side of the cold tub and stared.

Eventually it was full, and I stood in the middle of the tub and poured the mildly, warm water over my head and other parts of my body. I placed the bucket back under the faucet, and while it refilled, began to soap myself down and scrub. When I'd finished and the bucket was full again, I carefully poured the water over my body, as efficiently as possible to keep from repeating the process too many times and put the bucket back to once again rinse. I repeated the process until I felt reasonably clean and toweled dry. I HAD closed the window.

Finally, I got into my underwear and socks and shaved in relative comfort with dripping, lukewarm water, standing on a mound of warm towels. Think of it!

I decided I wouldn't say anything about it to Sting but maybe the butler. It would be days and many miles before I saw MY shower again. The one with all the pressure.

I went back to my room and dressed in sweat pants and a pullover sweater, then went to Andrew's room and gently tapped on the door. "Hey, Love," I said, "time to go!"

"Comin," came the answer, and out he popped looking like he'd slept all night and ironed his clothes. He's like that.

This time when we came down, we noticed that a large dining table had been set up in the main entrance hall. Beautiful stuff, I thought. Boy, I'm hungry!

On either side of the entry hall were large rooms used for dens or living rooms, I guess, each with mammoth fireplaces, and in the one on the left, the portable control center was set up. At the controls were world-famous producer, Hugh Padgham, co-producing with Sting, and engineer Simon Osburn. Sting sat on a barstool in front of the console, and they were listening to a tune I liked immediately, *Let Your Soul Be Your Pilot*. As it turned out, it was the first song Sting wanted to work on. And it was in the key of F#(sharp)! One of the worst keys for horns and us jet-lagged and hungry.

Good smells were wafting in from the kitchen as Sting ushered us through the entrance hall once again, past the dining table and into the other huge room off to the right of the main hall. There, set up for us, were microphones (three Neumann U-87's, our favorites) and headphone playback systems. We got our horns out, put them together and blew a little to make sure what key the song was in. Ooh, well!

Thank God this song was in fairly straightforward format (an arrangement of beats in a bar of music). Nothing foreign or unusual there. Regular eight bar phrases, one after the other, and the chorus' were merely the same format in a different key.

Sting has some ideas for when the horns should come in and what they should play, and we listened patiently, beginning to figure out his style of communication. He mentioned the word "Stax" quite often, and we knew what he wanted. We always sound like we did back then anyway, so it wasn't any trouble. We didn't say that though.

Before an hour was out, we had all the sax solos done on the song, and he was looking happy again.

Luckily for us, the butler came in and quietly said to Sting that the meal was ready, and the guests were assembled. Good! I was starting to shake, and Andrew was getting there, too. It was time for us to eat!

This time when we arrived at the dining table, three candelabras and other indirect lighting softly lit the room. There was a respectful round of applause as we followed Sting to the head of the table. He introduced us to his very pregnant and still radiant wife, Trudie, and their current three; Mickey, Jake and Coco. She directed me to take the empty seat next to her, and Sting indicated that Andrew sit next to him, directly across from me. At the other end of the table in the seat of honor was Hugh, the producer, surrounded by four musicians on one side and four engineering or technical staff on the other. Sixteen diners altogether.

A man in a white jacket appeared and began going around with two bottles of wine. A red and a white and offering it to everyone. Andrew and I had the red and asked for water, which came moments later.

Then it was time for small talk, and we told of our trip over, our families back home and my marriage to Amy and how we met. That brought some laughs and catcalls.

When the glasses were half-empty, the butler walked up to Sting and asked, "Sir, will you be served?"

Andrew and I were caught off guard, but to our credit, never cracked a smile, although we'd never seen this kind of tradition before.

He looked down at his fingernails for an instant and said, "Served, thank you."

Women dressed in black aprons with lace trimming began to pour out of the kitchen with steaming platters of delicious smelling foods. Each stopped at Sting's chair first and put whatever amount he indicated on his plate. Then on to Trudie and the children, then down to the rest of us in turn.

There was a platter of fish followed by one of chicken and then a beautiful ham surrounded by sweet potatoes. Then rice and other vegetables came and circled the table. What a feast it was! The wine in my glass never reached the bottom, as there always seemed to be someone at my elbow with another bottle.

It was quiet for awhile after everyone got started, then Trudie began to ask about our families and how many kids we had. That gave Andrew his break, and he got to talk for a long time. Then I told as much as I dared to strangers about mine. They got the idea though, we were very proud of our kids.

Sting suddenly asked, "And will you leave them and go on the road with us?" He is obviously a master of timing.

Andrew and I stopped eating. And I must have blushed, because Trudie laughed. I looked over at Andrew, and he was smiling and nodding his head in the affirmative. So I said, "I don't see why not. We'd love that!" We got more applause, and Sting looked satisfied.

There was a lot of good-natured banter back and forth between the players and crew. Andrew and I were too far apart to have much to say, and we were busy eating. Usually, Andrew shows more restraint than I do in these situations, but tonight he was getting it on pretty well!

Then Sting said, "And may I ask how it was being with Elvis Presley?"

The others quieted, and I was on the spot since Andrew doesn't normally like to discuss Elvis. Hell, he doesn't even display the gold album he got for the work. I've never asked why.

Trudie said, "Yes, do tell!"

So I began. I talked for about thirty minutes about Memphis and the music starting in the Sixties, jumping from story to story as they came to my mind, a lot about Elvis and the Mar-Keys. Our trips to his house and the fairgrounds seemed to really please them. At one point, Andrew said, "Tell the one about Otis and the plane crash."

But Sting vetoed that. "Wait a minute, boys," he laughed, "there's always tomorrow night! That was great, but we've got to go to work now!" He threw down his napkin and backed his chair away from the table, getting up and stretching.

We all followed suit, and I gave Trudie a hug before leaving the table and catching up with Andrew.

Andrew at The Lake House, Sting's home

Had I known about the next song, *I Hung My Head,* I wouldn't have been so anxious. But first we had to finish *Let Your Soul Be Your Pilot.* What a pleasure this song was. So melodic and inspiring with a captivating lyric. In about two hours, we had done all we could to it and went to the control room to hear the results. Sting was all smiles, as were the technical staff. Andrew and I were pleased as well.

So Sting said "onward," and Hugh cued up the next track. It came booming over the big speakers, and my scalp tingled as I realized fatigue could make a fool of me tonight. That's your worst fear, you know, riding in on the white horse of your reputation and falling on your ass as you try to dismount right in front of the boss.

At first, I thought it was the jet lag. The time signature kept changing around like a crazy wind. First this and then that, and the line he gave us didn't seem to fit where he sang it. Guess what key it was in, too? You got it! F#! I hung my head.

We've been in all kinds of situations, but this was the worst. So tired I could hardly hold my eyes open, and Sting was energized beyond belief. He is a great musician, and I was beginning to wonder if he'd ever been fatigued.

As we forged on into the night, we began to "get it." It wasn't really that hard, just tricky to tired minds. Sting was directing us in, and it helped. So we made headway.

After that song was finished, he sat on his stool in the control room having listened to a very loud playback and said, "That's good. We'd better get some rest. Big day coming. I've got to go into London early in the morning for some promotion matters, so why don't you fellows do some sightseeing. I'll let you have a car and driver. We'll have two more songs tomorrow and some filming for a TV special. By the way, I love what we've done tonight! Rest well."

We hugged and shook hands, but Andrew and I didn't linger to talk. We dragged ourselves up the stairs and managed to say goodnight to each other before going into our respective rooms and falling out! I'm not sure what time it was locally, but in my body, it was mid-afternoon with no sleep the night before. I slept like the dead for a little while, then fitfully after that and was up early.

This time, I opted for a soaking bath. I turned the hot water on all the way and let it run the whole time I was shaving. When I finally got in the tub, there were a few inches of water in it and that, only warm. It did fine though, and I kept the black bucket under the faucet filling all the time to rinse. It was better, although the English mornings always seem chilly, and I was glad to finally be dry, clean and dressed.

We had breakfast in the kitchen at another nice, long table attended by John the butler. He just asked what we'd like, and it seemed anything was possible.

After we'd finished, he informed us our car and driver were waiting outside. We crunched our way over to a big, black Daimler sedan and found the doors already open.

"Good morning, sirs," began the driver, "anything in particular you'd like to see this morning or would a spin around the countryside do?"

"We'd like to ride through the country and wind up at Stonehenge," I replied.

"Very good, sir. We'll start with a drive into the hamlet of West Amesbury."

We left the Lake House and drove on a curvy, English two-lane road obviously not meant for two cars. Our driver told us about the inhabitants of many cottages and larger estates along the way. Then we passed the inevitable country pub that he said the guitar player visited every night late, and he'd have to retrieve him. The English are not snotty about drinking or even getting drunk for that matter. And anyway, it was the guitarist.

We stopped in the charming, little village and got out to take a few

Wayne at Stonehedge

pictures and stretch our legs a bit. It was warm in the car but cool outside, and I was glad I'd brought my jacket. The town was so clean and neat in the brilliant sunlight I wanted to stay and look around, but Andrew was inclined to push onward. And anyway, we'd been cold in English towns before. I think Andrew wanted to be back in his bed at the house, and it wasn't a bad idea.

But I'd always wanted to see the ancient monument, Stonehenge, and never made it. So I pleaded my case, and Andrew relented. Nice of him since I'm not sure how really interested he is in ancient white man stuff.

Standing there in the middle of the Salisbury Plain next to the Druid mystery, I gazed around and saw the burial mounds within the two-mile radius. What really went on here, I wondered. And why did Sting decide he wanted to live within two miles of this five-thousand-year-old powerful place? He has an aura of mystery about him, and I hoped I'd have a chance to ask him about it someday. Maybe he was a priest here in the long ago!

When we got back to Lake House, the television people were setting up, and Sting was in the control room already listening to the first song we were to do that afternoon.

"Grab some food, and let's get to work. We've loads to do!" he said in cheerful anticipation.

We trooped hungrily down to the kitchen and found a platter of sandwiches. All the English favorites; watercress, cucumber, butter and

Wayne and Andrew at Sting's studio

cheese. There was even a paper-thin slice of ham on some of them. Butler John asked if we were thirsty, and we took water. Cokes in England are loaded with caffeine and will rob you of needed sleep.

Then back to the microphones. Sting had another surprise waiting for us. He was strapping on a tenor sax when we arrived! He laughed, and said it was a secret fantasy of his to blow with the Memphis Horns.

They had the song, *You Still Touch Me*, ready, and we worked up the very nice and simple horn lines with Sting and began recording.

Guess what? He has a really nice sound on that thing.

We had a ball, and there was laughing all over when we listened back in the control room. Hugh quipped, "You've missed your calling, Sting, now you'll be leaving us and moving on over to Memphis!"

"No," he said. "They'll be moving over here!" More genuine laughter.

The television crew was now all around us filming everything about the session. Good thing they had powerful lenses, or they would have been right up in our faces.

So Sting says, "Okay then, we'll do the interviews before dinner, and we've got one more tune after that." We interviewed together and alone in another huge room with a roaring fire and loads of TV equipment.

This time as I entered the main hall for dinner, I began to notice courthouse-sized paintings of men dressed in period clothing and wondered if they came with the house. Maybe they were of Sting's distant ancestors. It was something else I was anxious to ask him about.

We sat in our appointed spots once again, and this time, when Butler John approached the lord of the manor with his nightly question, Sting replied, "I think tonight we will buffet, please."

And again, the long line of ladies dressed in lace-trimmed, black aprons came pouring out of the kitchen with their steaming trays, but this time they marched by us and deposited their delightful loads on the long buffet table that ran the length of the wall. Sting and his family rose from the table and began at one end, filling their plates from the large selection. Then the rest of us stood and began filing past the food line helping ourselves to the tempting array of dishes. Like before, there were four meats and several veggies, all smelling wonderful. It was so cool.

The questions tonight began coming from all over the table, not just from Sting. It was like the first night was to honor us, and tonight was a free for all! For an hour we talked of Stax artists and Atlantic ones, too. Otis, Aretha, Ray Charles and King Curtis. Al Green, the fabled Willie Mitchell, Otis Clay. The stories rolled on and on, and the company could hardly get enough. Of course, I love telling the familiar stories of my life. That is what I've done all my life. Have adventures with stars, all while building a reputation like nobody else in music history. I've just had fun, which is what every musician hopes to do while making a pretty good living at the same time!

And here Andrew and I were at another powerful singer's home, at his table, repeating all the stories that everybody loves to hear. It's like a trademark, in a way, although the Memphis Horns' sound is really our thing.

Sometime during the meal in a lull of the constant buzz, I leaned over to my left and asked Trudie, "Would you mind telling me who is in the big, oil painting right behind Andrew?"

It showed two men at a table, one holding a scroll and the other with paper in front of him holding a writing instrument, obviously a scribe, both dressed in beautiful robes. Behind them a white column stood backed by trees and blue sky. It had its own beautiful light.

"I don't know for sure. I think it's a magistrate that lived in the last century. At any rate we inherited it with the house and love it, so there it hangs."

Not the romantic answer I'd hoped for but a good answer.

Her eyes were bright, and she was very friendly, obviously having a grand time. I decided I liked her a lot.

Everyone was eating Euro style, forks upside-down to ours, and knives held like a knife fight. Their way looks more practical. Our way must be the different one. I was trying for my best table manners, since I tend to eat like an animal if not corralled by Mother or Amy. Andrew, on the other hand, is a gentleman with great manners at all times.

The meal finally wound down, and Sting threw his napkin on the table to signal the time had come to return to work. Everyone backed their chairs out and rose to leave.

"Get up *Four Seasons*, Hugh. Let's take a look at that. Last one of the day."

"Sounds good," said Hugh, departing the table for the control room.

"Well," said Sting, looking right at us. "I shall leave you to your own devices on this one. Need I say I hope you'll go to Stax for me this time." He grinned hugely at this remark, and we all rose and started making our way to the microphones.

"No problem on that one," said Andrew, and I laughed.

I was glad to have the opportunity to show off a little. We've always done our best work when left alone with the song. Our job does include making both the artist and producer happy at the same time, but when we make ourselves happy we help them make hit records.

Four Seasons was made for us. Kenny Kirkland did a masterful job on the B-3 organ, as did Vinnie Colaiuta on drums. Dominic Miller sounded just like Steve Cropper for this song, and Sting's bass was perfectly Memphis. The words and feel were very reminiscent of Memphis, too. It really cooked.

We unabashedly took horn lines from our own repertoire. Lines from songs Sting himself had mentioned. They were specific, too. He said, "like *Mr. Pitiful,*" more than once. He, like so many others, love that stuff from Stax, and we do, too. Hell, that's how we've made our living!

So it was a joyous ending to a lovely day in English paradise. We gathered in the control room and listened to all the music we'd done one more time at full volume. Sting stood with his hands stuffed down in his pockets, blond head bobbing up and down, grinning like a little boy with a shiny, new, Christmas toy. The control room was out of control when we finished, slapping backs, shaking hands and laughing. We got hugged a lot by people saying how they couldn't wait to get on the road with this music.

Us, too!

As things began to calm down, Sting put his arms around our shoulders like two long lost brothers and gently ushered us out to the main hall, then paused to have a private moment. He smiled back and forth at us.

"So, it's settled then. We'll see you in New York for rehearsals after the first of the year I should think."

"Yes, yes," we chorused, "we'll be there with bells on!"

"Now, it's off to bed for you. I'm afraid we've stayed up rather late. John should be at your door around five for breakfast call, and your car will take you to London at six. Sleep well and have good travel!"

We went to our rooms, and when I lay down in my bunk, I was grinning like a possum up into the darkness. I'm not sure I quit grinning even when I went to sleep. We'd done it again! We were in like flynn!

Sleep didn't last long, though. Along about four-thirty, a soft knocking came at my door, and Butler John's voice said, "Sorry, sir, breakfast in twenty minutes."

Then I heard him down the hall at Andrew's door.

I rushed to the bathroom, brushed my teeth, shaved and splashed water under my arms. I wasn't about to do the shower thing again. I put on plenty of deodorant and after-shave. Then I threw my things in my bag and went to Andrew's door. "You ready, man?"

"Just a second," he replied. "I'm comin'."

And like I always do, I said, "Okay, I'll meet you down in the kitchen." This usually hurries him along a bit. Usually.

He met me soon after I sat down. Butler John came over to the table dressed in his black pants and starched, white shirt, but this time with an apron on. He would personally cook our breakfast!

We ordered eggs and bacon and so forth, normal fare, and Butler John began serving muffins and hot tea.

When our food was in front of us, he stood by the table and did something I'd never seen. He buttered our toast!

And when he'd finished that, he asked ever so politely, with a lilting voice, "Jam?" I was stunned, but I managed, "please."

He took the knife and with much style and flourish, spread jam liberally on my buttered toast.

He did the same with Andrew, and I could tell the black man from the Delta enjoyed the process immensely. I can only imagine his thoughts as the English gentleman's "man" served him his breakfast like a king. He was smiling down at his plate, rubbing his hands together and looking up at me with his big, brown eyes.

We always do enjoy ourselves!

While we were eating, Butler John took our horns and bags out to the waiting Daimler sedan we'd used the previous day to expedite matters. Then we showed up, and he warmly shook hands with each of us. "Do come back again soon, sirs, and have a very fine voyage home!" he said with all sincerity.

"We will, and thank you for everything," we replied as we got in the back of the car.

We began crunching our way down the gravel drive for the last time, and I looked back to see Butler John standing on the top step, grinning and waving a large, breakfast napkin over his head to us. We smiled and waved back.

As we climbed up onto the main blacktop road leading to the big highway, I looked back one more time, and there was Butler John still standing on the top step to the house, waving his big goodbye to us. I was really touched, but maybe he was just glad to be rid of the Yankees at last!

It was a long ride back to London from the Lake House, and we were glad to get there and stand up while we went through the same process in reverse. Then after an hour or so wait, we climbed aboard the mother ship for the flight back home. An all day affair.

We rumbled down the runway and lifted up over the lush, green, English countryside, shaking and rattling our way over the Irish Sea before attaining a smoother altitude. I don't even mind the shake, rattle and roll anymore. In fact it kind of makes me drowsy now, and soon I was drifting off into a nice half-sleep. But I knew that beside me it was another story. Andrew's black knuckles had turned white from clutching the armrest, as they always do in a little turbulence.

My mind began to travel back to the dinner table where the stories were flying. I thought about the experience I'd just lived through and wondered how many people on planet Earth would have liked to have shared it with me.

Untold numbers, I thought. I thought of all the stories I'd told and how much the company had enjoyed them. And I thought about how much I had enjoyed telling them!

A new thought was forming in my mind.

Later that evening when I got home to my Amy, I relayed what I'd been thinking. She laughed quietly and nodded, yes, pointing upstairs to our small office with the big desk and computer.

After unpacking and taking care of my just-home business, I found myself seated before the dark screen and flicked it on.

Then I began to write.

* Sadly, there was no Sting tour for us, but that's another story.

Across The River To Memphis

I've been writing these stories since that day I returned from England, and it's been fun remembering the things that made me laugh, taught me, built me up and tore me down and finally made me the man I am today. It's hard to believe that the same kid who couldn't get it together to graduate high school wound up forty-five years later at Sting's dinner table telling stories from his life!

I hear myself telling parts of them to interviewers from different media around the world, according to the questions they asked, and it is interesting that so many things could happen in one lifetime to a kid across the river from Memphis. So today, sitting around the Memphis condo I share with wife, Amy, and pup, Gracie, I thought this would be as good a time as any to put it all together, once and for all, in book format.

After all, I am seventy now, and urgent is more a feeling than a word.

It's been sixty-four years since I told my Grandmother Jackson something from that mystery place where prophetic sayings come from. I was the last one leaving her house in Jackson, Mississippi, holding the screen door open with my foot, when she leaned down, looked into my deep, green eyes and asked, "Wayne, what are you going to do when you grow up?"

"Grandma," I said, "I'm going to be on the radio!"

And boy, was I ever!

I was born the first child of Edna Mai and Giffin Jackson at Baptist Hospital in Memphis, Tennessee, November 24th, 1941. After the customary one-week stay, they packed me up and headed west across the automobile side of the Harahan Bridge into the rich, Delta, cotton land of Northeast Arkansas.

Our home was in the little town of West Memphis, four miles from the western shore of the mighty Mississippi River on Highway Seventy, which ran from there to Little Rock and beyond.

West Memphis had started life as a fruit stand on a long, dirt road. Like most roads in those days, it was either a sea of choking dust or a sea of slippery, sucking, gumbo mud. The fruit stand sat at the intersection of Highway Seventy and Missouri Road. Missouri Road ran north and south. If you went north six miles, you'd get to Marion, the county seat. A few

Wayne Lamar Jackson

miles east, you'd come to a river town called Mound City, named for the Indian burial mounds located nearby, the remnants of an Iroquois civilization that long ago fled the white man's killing sticks and strange diseases.

At the eastern end of Highway Seventy was the Mississippi River, and the ferryboat that took everybody and everything across.

Local farmers got together and decided they needed a cotton gin at about the same spot as the fruit stand, so up one went. And in the South, where there was a cotton gin, there was a liquor store, a Baptist Church and a mule auction. Then they built another liquor store and another church, and the battle for dollars and souls began along Highway Seventy in what would become my hometown.

These new people and their families needed homes to live in and a store. So on came the builders and real estate salesmen, schools and used car lots, teachers and preachers, and people to sell clothes.

The black folks who were leaving the sharecropping system because of the four-row cotton picker moved in on the east side of the railroad tracks, south of Highway Seventy, in small frame and clapboard houses.

The white folks moved in west of the tracks and north of Seventy into brick and mortar homes and big, white, frame houses with picket fences near the new, Chevy car dealership.

These people were poor to middle income families, but much richer than the ones on the other side of the tracks. They worked at the cotton gin, the

Edna Mai holding Wayne

mill, the crop dusting service and some of them were farmers come-to-town.

I was born into all this just before Pearl Harbor, when West Memphis had become a little, seven-mile stretch of liquor stores, car lots and churches of all denominations, except Jewish. There were enough people of that "other" faith to allow one Catholic Church and school. There were attendant business services by now, a small police force headed by Chief Bud Holland, Dr. Hamilton who made house calls and Spott's Drug Store to deal aspirin and dispense the medicine Dr. Hamilton prescribed.

And don't let me forget the two cotton gins and Dacus Lumbermill and Casket Company, by far the biggest industries.

The traffic was moderate coming and going across the Harahan Bridge to Memphis all the time but could be heavy on the weekends, because after dark in West Memphis, you could drink, gamble and whore on Eighth Street in "colored" town. There was cock fighting, dog fighting and something called, "Coon On A Log." Nasty business of a hound dog trying to get a coon off a log in the shallows of the river. A stopwatch was involved in some way. Very nasty business allowed on the west side of the river in Arkansas but not on the east side in Tennessee. Sometimes I think they let that go on just to give the politicians of the era something to yell about on election days. Daddy owned a funeral home on Tenth Street and did a right good business just off the residue from all that weekend funnin'. He said a weekend on Eighth was good for two or three killings anytime.

In addition to the funeral home, Dad sold life insurance for Reliable Life, and Mama worked at Guaranty Loan and Real Estate. We were middle-row Methodists and lived on the crest of Sand Hill, the highest spot in town, at number 325 Roosevelt, named after the President. When the Mississippi River overran its banks every other spring or so, trying its dead level best to make West Memphis a mud hole, the water never came closer than three or four blocks from us before stopping its perilous climb and starting to slowly recede, leaving everybody else in stinking muck over their shoes. Once when I asked an ancient black woman who ran a used shoe store down on Seventh Street what she remembered most about early West Memphis, she answered, "Mud. Mud mostly, and drunk niggers."

I guess that's why they decided to pave the streets, not to stop the drinking, that would have been impossible, but to hold off the mud so the drinking men could get to the liquor store.

The years went slowly by in that easy Arkansas manner, scorching summers and frigid, muddy winters. Then five years later my brother, Bruce, joined me. By that time I had gone through kindergarten in Mrs. Eaton's class at the First Methodist Church on Missouri.

After that incident at Grandma's house, I got my first guitar, and life was good. I was learning guitar chords from Gary, the Church of Christ minister's son, and loving it. I would sit by the radio and try to fit what I had learned into what was happening in the song. And I sang my heart out. Our maid at the time was Cora. She'd come through the living room and catch me at it and say, "My, my, ain't you sumthin'!"

Until I was around six, our house was one street south of the actual cotton fields. Then they started building the new high school across from the Shipman's house on Barton, right behind us. Just through our backyard, progress was in motion, and they began paving the streets. I loved the smell of melting lead and diesel fumes, sweating men and the roar of the big Cat D9 bulldozers. And I admit regretting the loss of all that gravel because of the friendly rock fights that seemed to always break out on the neighborhood streets, even though one escalated to bricks from which I carry a three corner scar on top of my head today.

Far from the smells of progress were the sweet scents of my backyard. Many a hot afternoon was spent lying in the grass, the air full of mint fragrance coming from the plants next to the old servant's quarters that was

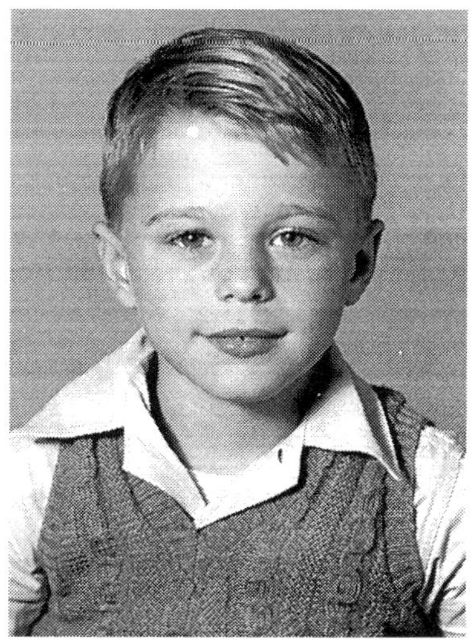

Wayne, age six

connected to the single car garage. Magnolia blossoms hung heavy in the trees and sweet honeysuckle wafted across the yard from the back hedge row, competing with the smell of frying chicken coming from Mama's kitchen.

There were no servants in the servant's quarters, but for awhile, it housed Aunt Dusty who was an operator for the West Memphis telephone company. Our number was one-one-three. A lady would answer any time you picked up the receiver and say, "Number, please." If you were a kid, you could just say who you wanted to speak to and that would do. Everybody knew everybody anyway, so usually they would call you by name.

As I said, the year I was seven, Mom and Dad gave me a Gene Autry guitar for Christmas. During the summer, it stayed in its black, cardboard case under my bed. However, on days when all the guys were down at the Cooper's stadium-sized, front lawn playing touch football, and I decided I didn't want to get my face squashed in the grass again, I'd sneak off to my house and get the guitar out. It was my friend and always ready to play. I strummed away many afternoons 'til my fingers were sore.

I liked to make up my own songs, as well as play along with the radio. I always tinkered around with words and when I did, I tingled. *One, Two, Buckle My Shoe*, was my first song. I thought it would be perfect for Johnny Cash. Little did I know, I'd actually work with him years down the road.

We didn't have a TV, so I was pretty focused. Lots of people didn't have TV, but Jerry Bledsoe, my best friend two houses down, had one. We often watched “The Mickey Mouse Club” together, and both of us fell in love with Annette Funicello. I loved “Space Cadets,” too.

We did have the radio, though, and it was always going. Mom loved the big band stuff, and she and her sisters danced around the house whenever they were together. They taught me to Jitterbug and Charleston. I loved it and would dance up and down the street singing *He's Got Personality* and *Sunny Side of the Street*, dreaming I was on the big stage!

Daddy, on the other hand, loved black, gospel music, and when I went with him on his debit we'd listen to that. We called on the black community out in the countryside mostly, and he sold thirty-five cents a week burial insurance, as well as life insurance. After I got a little older, I laughed at the thought of the insurance business and the funeral home together. Daddy NEVER cancelled a policy, and the customers generally wanted to be with Mr. Jack when the time came.

Poor folks in those days cooked and heated with coal oil, one step down from kerosene, and that's what we'd smell like when we came home at night. And maybe beer. Dad would usually stop for a couple of beers at Bill's Grill, a barbecue place out on the highway that connected Marion to West Memphis. I'd sit on the silver, spinning barstool next to him and have a coke, hoping he'd want a pack of Lucky Strikes. If he did, he'd give me the quarter to go get it for him. Each pack had three pennies in the side cellophane, and I got to keep those. Bubble gum was a penny apiece. I loved the white ones with Ford on them and the yellow ones, too. I'd get home with a big, fat jaw full of sweet, delicious chewing gum.

By this time, I was learning more songs. I could sing *Got Too Much Insurance* by Hank Williams, and it sure tickled everyone, especially Daddy. I learned *Darktown Poker Club* and *The Preacher And The Bear* by Phil Harris and could strum the guitar along with them. I didn't understand that there were racial connotations in those songs and wouldn't have been able to understand why anyway. I just knew they made people laugh.

They were the songs I won my first talent contest with down at the Avon Theater. It was raining that night when mother came to pick me up in the Desoto, tires hissing on the wet blacktop. I held the cardboard guitar case in one hand and my winnings in the other. I jumped in the front seat beside her and held up my one-dollar bill and four movie passes. “I won!” I cried, and Mom was duly impressed. She popped her gum and eyed me, “No kidding?”

Giffin and Wayne

And she was grinning.

"There's another one next week, and I joined it, too!"

From then on, I couldn't get enough of music and winning.

When we got home, Dad was sitting in his spot on the couch with his account book on his lap, smoking his pipe with his feet up on a wicker stool and gazing through the blue clouds of smoke. As I came in the back door, I waved my money and tickets at him and said I'd won them in a talent contest down at the movie house. He grinned and nodded, never taking his pipe from between clinched teeth. "Good," he chuckled, "you keep it up."

There'd never been a musician in the family before, and I don't think he took my music seriously. Well hell, neither did I, but I didn't take anything else seriously either. I thought I was Ricky Nelson. So I marched on back to my bedroom, slamming the door behind me and began wailing away like hell on that Gene Autry!

For boys, growing up in Arkansas meant growing up with guns. Hunting was a major preoccupation, as were outdoor sports of any kind. When I was eight, I wanted a Daisy Red Ryder BB gun like all the other big kids had, but Mama wouldn't hear of it. "Too dangerous," she said. However, on my twelfth birthday, Dad got me a twenty-two caliber, single shot rifle. He knew it was time I took responsibility for something. It was also my first "manly" thing, kind of like a rite of passage. It turned out I was a very good shot with the twenty-two. I took it quail hunting instead of a shotgun, like the other boys, and brought down more birds than they did. There were some things I excelled at naturally.

Swimming was another. I was between three and four years old when Marvin Demuth, the life guard at the tiny West Memphis Country Club (no golf course, but one tennis court), dropped me and Durrell Dallas off the diving board in the deep end for our first swimming lesson. We both dog paddled out just as naturally as two pups, and I became an avid swimmer. It was a good thing. I would need those swimming skills to navigate our other summertime watering hole.

We would ride our bicycles south across Broadway and east over to Seventh Street just one block from Eighth Street and "colored town." Although it would have been all right to go on over to Eighth Street and south again out to the garbage dump and the river, we never did, always imagining danger one more block over. The real danger, however, lay where we were headed.

The garbage dump was what I imagined hell to be like. Ours was a mountain of stinking trash, smoldering broken furniture, old tires, egg shells, orange peels, twisted metal, wrecked cars, mattresses and rotting food. Rats scurried to and fro between the mounds and made wonderful targets for the twenty-two caliber rifles that we carried to the dump rattling across the handlebars of our bikes. There were roads through and around the garbage, and we stalked the perilous foe at dusk after the big trucks stopped coming to disgorge their noxious loads. We wore cut-offs and T-shirts with sneakers or other rough shoes. When we'd had enough of the stink and smoke and shooting, we'd go over to the river and slide down the concrete revetment to the muddy water's edge.

On bright summer days, the Memphis skyline would stand out in bold relief, sitting high on its bluff across the rushing water. We'd sit on the revetment with long weeds sticking from between our teeth and stare silently as we dreamed our young dreams.

Now the Mississippi River is not called mean and mighty for nothing. It moves downstream towards New Orleans at about five or six miles an hour. At its edges, where the movement touches shore causing what are called eddies, it can suck a full-grown man down in an instant. Logs of tremendous size come down river after a rain and are partially underwater. If one hits you while your swimming, well it's all over. The thought of being skewered by a submerged branch still fills my gut with ice water. One can hit a small boat like a torpedo and break it to bits, instantly taking the broken boards and drowned bodies miles downstream before spitting them up.

It was into these waters that we hurled our young bodies, shouting and laughing about the current as we held onto shore-bound branches and each other to see how far out we could go. The ultimate dare was to actually swim the mile or so across to the other side. No one in our bunch ever tried, but there were some who did. And some even made it. Over the years though, on two occasions, the bloated, blue bodies of young boys were found surfaced miles downstream from where they started out, and a shocked community could not understand how such a thing could happen.

Finally, they banned the dump at the bottom of Seventh Street for everyone except city employees. We stayed away for awhile swimming in the bar ditches left by the spring floods instead. There, we only had to contend with water moccasins and old fishhooks.

I liked summertime adventures better than their wintertime counterparts. In winter, we trekked several miles across frozen cotton fields to get to "Rattlesnake Bottoms," a huge patch of woods left untouched since the beginning of time, loaded with squirrels, rabbits, coon and bob-cat. The winter was good there, because the rattlesnakes that the woods were named for slept through the cold.

Dad had a single-shot, long-barrel, twelve gauge recoilless shotgun he let me take on these trips. It kicked so hard I hated to fire it. If I aimed it up in a tree at a squirrel, for instance, it would almost turn me all the way around when I pulled the trigger, leaving a dark depression in my shoulder every time. It could reach to the top of a tall tree and get a squirrel though, and it made a good shot out of me. I never wanted to pull that trigger more than once at any given target!

Then there were the long, freezing walks home stepping in mud holes that could suck the goulashes right off your feet. Many times that gumbo just didn't want to give up. The tears would always run from my right eye down my face in that cold wind, and the snot down from my nose over my top lip. I could see our house way off in the distance not seeming to get any closer. "I'll never do this again," I'd swear to myself as I dug my chin further down in my wool scarf and my gloved hands deeper into my jacket pockets, long barrel twelve gauge hanging from the crook of my left arm. But I always did.

It was fun.

The only sport I didn't like was duck hunting. Getting up with Dad at four o'clock in the morning to go sit in a blind at the edge of some frozen lake waiting for a shot at a low flying duck was not my idea of fun. The grown men liked it, because they got to drink bourbon in the morning. But I got to where I would rather sleep longer and go to school. I think Dad was disappointed. After all, we did live in Arkansas. I heard him tell his buddies that I was going through a stage. They all agreed that it did happen.

Then I began to feel the same way about getting up at four o'clock to go fishing. The musician in me was surfacing when a ten o'clock date with the lawn mower seemed better than a four o'clock date with a fishing pole. Dad just shrugged.

I played junior high football and got in some games in the eighth grade matches. Dad loved football and came to watch me at the junior high school field. I think he was a little disappointed that I didn't do better, but all he ever said was, "When I played back in Helena, the boys were smaller." Like me, he was a short, wide man.

Fortunately, my brother, "Bruce the Large," was coming along and would one day avenge the Jackson clan on the field of honor, his senior class squad turning in an undefeated year making Dad and all of us very proud. Bruce was a natural jock, fixit-man and student. He was everything I wasn't, and it took the pressure off. I was free to let my mind fly far from the football field and duck blinds off into the galaxies of my science fiction books and into the land of show business.

Mother bought me a trumpet in my eleventh year from the Uptons who lived across the street, after their son, Dickie, had grown tired of it. I don't know why she did, but I think it came from that deep, down well of knowledge in mothers called intuition. Because for an eleven-year-old with nothing in his mind but happy thoughts, it turned out to be my Magic Wand! It was my math, my history, my English! And in the end, my diploma.

I think Mom and Dad had been playing cards over at their house that night. When they came home, Mom put a dull, black case on the dining room table. She opened it up and said, "Well, what do ya think of that?" I took one whiff of the light oil and pungent brass smells and got goose bumps. I looked at the velvet that lined the case and was excited in a way I couldn't describe. I picked the trumpet up and put the mouthpiece in. Then I got a deep breath and blew. It made a satisfying noise, in fact, a beautiful sound! I blushed, and Mom and Dad laughed. "I think he likes it," Dad said. He was right. And somehow I knew it wasn't exactly a toy.

From then on, I sat by the radio picking out chords on the guitar 'til my fingers hurt and melodies on the trumpet 'til my face hurt. Cora would beam. She was a fairly big woman, and when she laughed, it shook her all over. She'd wag her head and throw her hands up under her white apron, exclaiming, "Oh, that BOY!"

Doyne Dodd Sr. lived across the street from us. He was a professional trumpet player turned lawyer who had played his way through Tulane University and knew Louis Armstrong personally. Sometimes in the evenings, he would go upstairs in their house and practice his horn. He played all the older Dixieland tunes. I would lie in the ditch in front of our house, which was catty-corner to theirs, and listen to him as the moon rose and the clouds scudded by. One day when I was outside doing something or other, Doyne stuck his head out the door and said, "Hey Wayne, get your horn and come on over."

I did.

He taught me *Muskrat Ramble*. Then every once in awhile, he'd ask me back over and would teach me some more. I was a quick learner, and later Doyne was proud to say he'd taught me everything I knew!

I was also taking trumpet lessons at school and kept that up until I reached the eighth grade. Then I began band in the new high school on Barton Street just behind the house. We were the West Memphis Junior High Band and from my seat in the band room, I could see the back of our house. I was getting pretty good by then, and the two senior high trumpet players were taking notice, coming by our practices to listen to me and getting a little nervous. They would open our door and lean against the jam with their arms folded. They were both tall fellows who tried to smirk, but the angst showed through. After all, I would be a ninth grader and in the band with them the following year. Mr. Vance would look out over the class, give a wry smile and hitch up his pants. Joe Bowen and Don Butler were tenth graders and had it sewed up for their junior year. But I made 'um nervous.

That summer came, and I teamed up with Methodist Church organist,

Bob Hobbs, a West Memphis high schooler who had always lived in our neighborhood, and drummer, Johnny Baugh. We named ourselves The Dizzy Three. *Cherry Pink And Apple Blossom White* by Prez Prado was a hit that year, and I could play it as good as ole Prez. So that was our song. We won several local talent contests with it and again, like everybody else, we loved winning.

Then we had added the guitar and vocal talents of Eddy Sherill, whose daddy was a riverboat pilot and gone most of the time. I learned about playing solos in their living room from playing my trumpet along with his guitar and vocals. Since he played guitar, we played in guitar keys. I learned to play in "bad" keys for trumpet but didn't know any better, so it wasn't hard. I'd just remember the melody and base a solo off that. It always worked and still does. We used the youth hall down at the Methodist Church to rehearse the band, and some of our friends would come by to dance and encourage us.

Now, we were The Dizzy Four and could play dances. Our first road gig was sixteen miles out in Crawfordsville, Arkansas, (way, way out in the cotton patches) to play at the community center for a local dance. It was a town of about six hundred folks (one stoplight) who were mostly farmers. That night a particularly beautiful farmer's daughter, Linda Christopher, caught my eye. During a break in our playing, I asked her to dance with me, and she did. All of a sudden, ideas of a different sort were forming in my mind. Thoughts that would drive me to work two jobs in order to buy a car.

The other thing I was drawn to as much as music was flying. My love of it had started when I was around seven. One of my mother's sisters, Marion, had married an aviator who taught crop dusting at Ole Miss and owned and operated Fletcher Field in Clarksdale, Mississippi. It was about sixty miles by air from there to West Memphis, so he flew over many a Saturday and flew me and Mom back to Clarksdale for a visit, then home Sunday. He came in a Stinson Station Wagon single-engine, light plane, and I sat up front with him and "drove" over and back. I got hooked. Ben talked aviation to me the whole time, and I soaked it up like a sponge.

At home, I could ride my bike the six or eight blocks down Avalon Street to the intersection of Highway Seventy where Joe Bowen Sr. owned and operated Bowen Field. It was for crop dusters, but privately owned planes were kept there, too.

I'd sneak up to the planes parked along the line and just look inside. If I found one open, I'd get in and sit there toying with the controls, making buzzing noises. They were mainly Piper PA-18 crop dusters, and they always reeked of last season's dust or liquid poisons. I grew to love those particular smells. I still get excited when I smell defoliant from some guy's hopper spraying near the road I'm driving on. Sometimes I pull over and just watch, smell and smile.

I think Mr. Bowen knew what I was doing but never said anything. There's something magical about the sights, sounds and smells of an airfield that cannot be denied and are magnetic to little boys so inclined. I'm sure most pilots have had similar experiences like that. Drawn like a magnet to the machines that can take you into the wild, blue yonder!

One day I was minding my own business with my head way off in the clouds when I heard a high, nasal voice say, "Hey, Wayne! You havin' a good time?"

I was snatched back to earth instantly, and there stood Mr. Craig Tennison, a prominent West Memphian and a member of our church. He owned Tennison Steel and had been a destroyer officer during World War II. I thought I was busted and stuttered, "Yeah, I guess so. Hope I didn't hurt anything!"

"Naw, naw," he reassured me. "Wanna take a ride in my new Tri Pacer?"

"Sure," I blurted out.

"Well, meet me at noon Saturday, and we'll get you started."

Between Uncle Ben, Craig Tennison and the rest of the pilots at Bowen Field, I began to get quite a bit of flight time and most of it instructional. Dick Zerby took me up in his Stearman N17 and introduced me to inverted flight and aerobatics. They all thought I would follow in their footsteps, and they might have been right if fate hadn't intervened. During the summers, I pumped gas and ran the radio. Al Paudert, by then operator of Bowen Field, also let me taxi dusters up to the pumps to fuel and back to tie down. I was having a ball!

Back at school, it was tenth grade, and in the high school band, I was teamed up with seniors Joe Bowen Jr. and Donald Butler. We did the trio versions of *Bugler's Holiday* and *A Trumpeter's Lullaby*. We were so good that Mr. Vance had us play out in front of the whole orchestra at assembly, and we were a smash!

Director Phil Vance and Wayne

We won a high school contest and were invited to perform at the state level tryouts. We received the First Place Blue Ribbon! Mr. Vance had us playing all over the place, and we were very proud of our accomplishments. We traded places in the first chair trumpet position all year and enjoyed the tryouts. Although they had two years on me, I was pushing hard from behind and had one thing on them...I didn't study. All I did was practice and work and try to get to Crawfordsville.

Me and Ed Greer Garrett were sacking groceries a few afternoons a week at Mr. Kennedy's Big Star. Ed Greer's sister was Miss Arkansas in 1957, and his mother looked like a movie star. His daddy drank a lot though, and when the divorce came, Mr. Kennedy somehow got Mrs. Garrett out of the deal. Mr. Kennedy was a short, balding man, and he looked happy, puffing his big cigar and driving around town with the new Mrs. Kennedy in his long, shiny, Cadillac Seville.

Ed Greer and I almost never spoke of this. We were too busy with our own tenth grade lives, and we knew all that stuff at his house was gonna come to a no good end. We just stood back and watched it all in wonder.

There was some drinking at my house, too, and when Daddy got too much and felt bad about something, he could get loud. He and Mom would holler back and forth and scare us kids. We'd go in the bedroom, shut the door and get behind our beds. They got along well most of the time, though, but I heard Mama tell Cora once that she would divorce Giffin if she could take care of us kids. In those days, it was hard for a woman with children. Unless, of course, there was a Mr. Kennedy in the wings.

Except for those rare moments of alcoholic terror, we had a happy raisin' up on Roosevelt Street. Especially after sister, Sara, five years behind Bruce, came along and Mother would have no nonsense in the house. Dad was a good guy after all and loved us, but he DID like his bourbon, too. After Sara's arrival, he would down the last of his drink in the car, one foot out on the driveway and one in the car, then come in, eat his stovetop dinner and fall asleep at the kitchen table. Maybe he'd make it to the couch and fall asleep there, but after awhile I'd sneak up and touch him saying, "Don't you think it's bedtime?" I was never afraid of him. I just felt bad he didn't make it to bed.

Daddy had started a life insurance company called Cotton States Life there in West Memphis and had all the people needed to receive his charter. He was to be in Little Rock for the entitlement, but since he thought his proxy votes were all he needed, he stayed home to take care of the budding business. He never suspected that then Governor Cherry would cancel the proxy vote behind his back and ruin his opportunity to enter the insurance business at the ground floor level.

I learned that story from Mother many years later, and now I think that's what all the drinking was about. This also started my long and abiding mistrust of all politicians, although in the end I've learned that it is, after all, ALL about that.....politics.

So I did my homework sometimes and had help from Cecil Ferris. She walked me home from school everyday and was interested in me passing, Lord knows why. She was John Ed Ferris' girlfriend, and he was a very good friend of mine. He was the school photographer and developed his own photos in a lab in the garage of their house, a few blocks from mine. I thought he was a genius.

Soon I had saved three hundred dollars to buy the '51 Plymouth from a friend of Moms. It was a four-door sedan, black, six-cylinder straight stick on the column. It was my chariot. Best of all it had a large back seat, and the radio worked.

I had just turned sixteen and gotten my driver's license, and I was forbidden to drive outside the city limits. So I immediately began going to Crawfordsville to court Linda.

One of my best friends was Lynn Moore. He played baritone horn in the band and dated a girl named Sharon who also lived in Crawfordsville. It was double trouble. We both started smoking, and the girls did, too.

This was all going on in the second half of the tenth grade. It seemed time stood still with all the intrigue and fun we were creating! I was in love and winning contests at the state level and talent contests at home and at the Mid-South Fair. I was flying Craig's Tri-Pacer and whistling my way through sacking groceries in the afternoon. I wanted for not and felt the glow of total, teenage infallibility. I even passed all my courses that year. Well, I passed, but by the grace of God, and Mrs. Hubble's wish to move me out of higher math.

I can thank Jimmy Shipman for my attitude about math. He was the kid, one year older than me, who lived in the house that backed up to ours and faced Barton Street. He went to the Catholic school and told me how hard all that math stuff was. And since he was a hero of mine, I believed him.

Soon, eleventh grade was looming on the horizon, and for some nutso reason I signed up for second year Algebra. You can imagine Mrs. Hubble's horror. I'm still confused about doing that. Maybe because I would stand at the stove in the evenings as Mom cooked those wonderful dinners, and we'd talk about what I wanted to be when I grew up. The only thing I could think of was a pilot, because I loved it so. She'd say, "Well, if you want to be a pilot, you'll have to be good in math!" Music didn't even enter the conversation. There simply was no way to use it to make a living.

So that may have had something to do with it. But I wasn't using math in the Tri-Pacer, just flying.

The Dizzy Four entered a series of talent contests and won them all. We found ourselves in the finals of the Mid-South Fair talent contest. Contestants came from all over, and the excitement was huge. The winners were to go on the nationally televised "Ted Mack Original Amateur Hour" as a contestant with the grand prize being a chance at a career in show business.

We played our hearts out and came in second, being beat out by a well-endowed, blonde, female singer. Oh well, we were stars at home for that day anyway.

My time was divided between school, music, working at the store and trying to get to see Linda. Lynn Moore, Randy Jones (who's dad had been a big band trumpet player and mom had been the girl singer), and I worked hard at not doing right!

In small town Arkansas in the Fifties, life went one of three ways. If your

Linda and Wayne

parents were well off and if you had the high school grades, you went away to college. Or you graduated high school, got married and went in business with your dad (usually farming). Or you just got a job and went up in the ranks of that job, if you could.

I don't know why, but Linda and I decided to get married soon after 1957 began. On Mother's Day, May 11th, we eloped to Senatobia, Mississippi, about fifty miles south of Memphis, where a justice of the peace married us. Just like that. We did have back-up accomplices on the telephone in West Memphis to say they were our parents, and it was okay. WOW!

We drove back to West Memphis and went to Marcy and Cookie Marcellini's apartment to celebrate. They were good friends of ours and had gotten married in high school, too. We went into their guest bedroom for a little while, and then Marcy and Cookie brought in a big, banana pudding with a candle in it. The deed was done. We ate warm pudding and went back home, me to my parent's house on Roosevelt Street and her to her parent's house in Crawfordsville. It was late Sunday night, and we were at our separate schools the next day, sixteen miles apart.

I have not a notion of what we expected next. We went about our days as though nothing had happened. I flunked Algebra II by a mile. No reason to talk to Mrs. Hubble about it either. The final day, she clucked at me as she scratched her head with the single chopstick that stuck through her bun and said, "Wayne, you've got too many irons in the fire!"

And I did.

Summer came, and Linda got pregnant. I was working at the grocery store and at the airport, too, changing crop dusters over from spray to dust and learning more about it from the duster pilots every day. I really thought I would go their way. I liked their dare devil attitudes, beer drinking and constant partying. I thought they were cool, but they were just blowing off being scared of hitting power lines and sharecroppers' houses out in the middle of a patch.

Dick Zerby was flying me upside down in his Stearman, complete harness but no parachute, and it was way better than anything at the fairgrounds! I was getting used to it. Dick also took me on "stiff" trips where we took his beautiful Bonanza 35 model with the v-tail and flew human corpses for cargo around the southeast. With the back seat out, there was enough room for a stiff secured to a gurney and strapped in as cargo behind the left seat. He let me sit there, which was normally the pilot in command's place. And he sat in the right seat so he could let it all the way back and sleep as soon as we got off the ground and were set up on a homeward bound course. He usually needed a nap after the late hours he kept, so I was on my own 'til we got near let down. Then he'd come back to life, that is if he wasn't trying to pull one and pretend not to be able to wake up! I learned tons and had a ball!

School was close to starting, and we needed to tell our folks about all of this but were just plain chicken. Linda's older sister, Betty, knew all about it and volunteered to come over to our house and "inform" Mom and Dad. On a steamy Sunday in August after church, she arrived.

We all assembled in the living room, Betty on the edge of an armchair casually swinging her leg, Mom and Dad on the couch under the windows and Linda and I on the couch by the front door. I guess so we could get out fast if we had to!

"Mr. and Mrs. Jackson, Wayne and Linda have something they want to tell you," she said with a big smile. "They have eloped and are now married!" Linda and I were beet red.

Daddy pulled out his white, linen handkerchief, mopped his forehead, rose and left the room, muttering, "Ooh, God," as he went. He nearly tripped over Bruce, who was hiding around the corner in the dining room so he could hear everything.

Mother looked at Linda and smoothed the wrinkles of her skirt down with her beautifully, manicured hands, "Well, ahem, welcome to the family Linda," she managed to say, with the slight inclination of her head and a twitching, little smile. Then she got up and rushed to join Dad, wherever he had gone.

We moved into the boys' room, and Bruce moved into the den, where he slept on the couch for that whole year. At some point, when Daddy wanted his TV rights back, Bruce and Sara shared her room with a piece of tape down the center that neither party got to cross.

What fun Linda and I bestowed on the Jackson household!

But we made it. Week by week and month by month, time rolled by. I was intent on band, winning more medals at all-state tryouts and flunking senior English. I still worked at the grocery store when I could, but the money was slim. And Linda's delivery date was approaching. Mr. Vance, my band director and friend, saw an opportunity to help me, and he did.

Over in Memphis, there was an orchestra leader named Collie Stoltz. He was a friend of Phil's, and each year, he provided the music for the Mid-South Rodeo over at the fairgrounds. Phil explained my circumstances, and it was agreed that if I would join the Musicians Union, he would hire me for that gig. It cost fifty dollars, and you had to go in front of the Board. The president of Local Seventy-one was the father of a prominent West Memphis lawyer, Vince Skillman, and Vince's son, Chuck, was my brother's best friend. So one afternoon at the beginning of 1959, I went to the union hall and appeared before a group of older guys who had heard about my horny, little ways and snickered all the way through the swearing in and turning over of my fifty bucks. I was issued a card and have been a member ever since.

The rodeo was the last two weeks in February. I showed up every afternoon at two p.m. for the matinee and again at six for the evening show. First, we'd play the national anthem. Then each time a gate opened and some fool came bounding out of the stall on the back of twelve hundred pounds of smokin' hell, we'd play a little truffle intro reminiscent of *William Tell*, as the rider hit the ground, usually about five seconds later. We'd do it again and again...all afternoon and all night. Most of the other musicians were much older than this little high school senior. But they tolerated me, and we had some laughs. For this, I was paid thirty-six dollars a day. I had been making about eighteen dollars a week at the store, and after doing that math (which even I could handle), I decided mopping floors, sacking groceries and stocking shelves was not for me.

In ten days I had made three hundred and sixty dollars, enough money to bring my daughter, Carla, into this world! Wow! And had a ball doing it. I began whistling even more for some reason. And because I'd missed ten days for the rodeo, I couldn't catch up in bookkeeping and flunked flat.

In early March, Linda's water broke, and she was off to the hospital. On March 3rd, Carla Renee Jackson entered this world, and it was a happy occasion. Linda's parents were there, as well as mine. My best friend, Lynn Moore, and I showed up and held Carla. Lynn was dubbed godfather, and I was proud. But Linda was about to get the first taste of what was in store for her. Lynn and I announced we were off to the band competitions in Hot Springs and ran downstairs and jumped in his Daddy's new 1957 Plymouth Fury. We tore off down Highway Seventy towards Little Rock. How we did it, I'm not sure. But we made it in time for all the activities and competitions.

We did great in the tests, and I was chosen for first all-state band again! It was all very exciting, but in the back of my mind there was a tickle. What WAS I going to do?

Everybody loved Carla. She was truly a beautiful baby, with big, brown eyes and wispy, blonde hair. The grandparents loved to keep her, especially the Christophers who had more time since they were farmers.

We stayed on at the Jackson house with Bruce sleeping on the couch. I ran around West Memphis High trying to get good enough grades to pass the final exams, but I failed senior English. That left me with a deficit of three credits. There would be no diploma for me that year, although I was in the yearbook and had my senior ring. What I did, however, was be the featured entertainment in front of the orchestra for the graduation crowd, playing *Londonderry Air (Danny Boy)* and *Mr. Wonderful* and getting a thunderous, standing ovation while my classmates filed by and got their rolled-up white diplomas. I'm not sure which I would have rather had!

Out in the crowd, Daddy once again pulled out his white, linen handkerchief and mopped his brow. My uncle, Eddy Gene, later told me he said, "That boy will never make it."

Wayne age 18

I had been playing on weekends west of town on Highway Seventy at the Jungle Inn, a roadhouse where you could get a quarter beer, a steak and live music on the weekends. They also had a row of "cabins" out back, and I thought, gee, that's nice. A traveling man can just stop here, have dinner and some music and then go on out back and spend the night. How convenient!

I was born like that.

The band was Jim Climber "99 Pounds of Rock and Roll" and The Wildcats. Boy, he was skinny. I went to his house in Memphis once to rehearse and saw him in his underwear. It was scary. He looked like a series of toothpicks with apples for elbows and knees.

His baritone sax man was Les Brueck who had the *Rock Around The Clock* horn line written out in every key and would play it on every song. It was exciting to me, because we were playing a real joint. And we got a few dollars.

Soon school was out, and Daddy started worrying about what I was going to do. It was clear West Memphis did NOT need a trumpet player. Nor did it need any other skill I had acquired in my short life. And rodeos only happened once a year.

And did I say that I flunked the tryout for the Navy Band at the Navel Air Station in Millington? Oh, yeah, by a mile. Since we didn't have a jazz band at West Memphis High, I had not a clue about that kind of phrasing, and that's all they were interested in. Mr. Vance must have fronted me in pretty strong to get me that far. Commander Vanderhorn, who administered the tryout, suggested I go home and practice jazz phrasing until I was eighteen, then come back for another try. It was NOT a thrill.

So Dad and I decided to give the U.S. Army a shot at getting a red-hot trumpet player on their payroll. Dad's main aim, anyway, and we were off to the recruiting office.

The well-pressed and spit-shined Sergeant Major was glad to see us come in. He looked me up and down with an appraising eye. "Yes, yes, Mr. Jackson," he said, smiling hugely, "sit down and tell me about yourself!"

"Well," I started, "I'm married and have a new daughter named Carla." His eyes narrowed, but his smile never wavered.

"When did you graduate?"

"Well, actually, I need three more credits to get my diploma, and I was hoping to get the last credits while serving in the Army."

That seemed to perk him up, and he slid out a form from his desk drawer and licked the tip of his pencil.

"Let's get some basic information going on you then, Wayne," he said. "What's your date of birth?"

I told him.

He wrote it in the appropriate space and then stopped. He seemed to be thinking and turning a little red under the collar. A vein on his forehead stood out and throbbed. Then he raised his head and looked right at me.

"You're not eighteen years of age, are you?"

"Not 'til November twenty-fourth, sir."

I must say he kept his composure well after that. He stood up from behind his desk and extended his hand to Dad and me.

"I suggest, Wayne, that between now and the time you turn eighteen you somehow get those other three credits and the high school diploma that goes with it. It will bode well for you in this man's Army. We'll talk again then."

So there we were out on the hot sidewalk in the lovely, early June afternoon with nowhere else to go except home.

Dad looked at me and smiled. "Don't worry. We'll find something."

I did have an "in" with the National Guard that I hadn't thought of. Vince Skillman, whose father was president of the Musician's Union was also the Commander of the National Guard Unit in West Memphis. So we called up Captain Skillman, and he said the Guard would take me at seventeen with or

Wayne in the National Guard

without a high school degree. It would train me in a job skill, and in addition, keep me out of Vietnam! I didn't even know why that was important.

He said I could join right away, and we all got excited. I would have an occupation, and Linda would have the money wives got. When asked about music, he said I'd just have to take what the Army testing said I was adept in. It didn't matter, we thought, I'd at least wind up with an occupation out of the experience.

Right!

So, one morning in late July, I was up early and kissed my brother and sister, Mother and Daddy, wife and daughter goodbye. Then Mother drove me down to the West Memphis bus station on her way to work. I boarded a Continental Trailways bus full of other nervous-looking boys and off to Fort Campbell, Kentucky, we went.

We arrived in time to get a duffle bag, some clothes that didn't fit and boots that did. We were shorn of our pretty hair and given inoculations against every disease known to man.

After that we began a three-day battery of tests that included physical, mental and psychological exams, in written, oral, and multiple choice formats.

We swung from monkey bars, marched in line and waited in lines for everything from chow to shots. I met a guy from Helena, Arkansas, named Jimmy Snyder, and we became friends for life.

Then we started the up at five a.m. business and falling out in the company street. It was going to take the next nine weeks to evaluate our tests, and at the end of basic, they would tell us what our fates were to be.

It seemed like it was going to be fun in a strange, game-like way. A John Wayne adventure, but nobody told me about Sergeant Pollard, our platoon boss. I think that job must be a punishment for regular Army who don't make the cut, because they are all bitter and love screaming. Sergeant Pollard was NO exception.

Where we were, there were two things you could be. One was, R.A. or Regular Army. You would be on active duty for at least two years and might have to go where there was shooting, and people ate with chopsticks. The other was, N.G. or National Guard. You would be going home for good in six months, unless something really awful happened to the country. The N.G. were hated and constantly chastised by the R.A. and the drill sergeants.

Sergeant Pollard lost no time in finding something I did wrong and dubbing me his "SCREW UP!" Being short, my uniform didn't fit perfectly, and I never did learn how to make up my bed. This was enough to start the whole tragedy of our relationship.

Parts were fun, though, while out of range of Pollard's voice. Working along side big tanks and artillery pieces was like being in a movie and gave us something to talk about at night before we finally got a few hours sleep time. Stuff to write home about.

The nine weeks went by, and basic was over. On the final day, we were all standing around waiting on our results from primary testing, and I saw Sergeant Pollard standing on the barrack steps. I walked over and offered my hand, which he accepted, and I said, "Thanks, Sergeant Pollard."

He smiled at me in a gruesome sort of way and said, "Jackson, you'll probably wind up being a general!" And he laughed.

I heard names being called from the company yard and went over to get the news. When my name was finally called, I grabbed the envelope and tore it open. There it was in black and white. I was off to Fort Sill, Oklahoma, to learn the skill the Army would teach me to take back to West Memphis, Arkansas, to enrich the rest of my life and the community's...Artillery Survey/ Forward Observer.

Possibly the most dangerous job ever devised by man in warfare and totally useless at home, unless they decided to defend Kroger from the Vietnamese with Howitzer 105s.

To make it more interesting, it was a job driven by higher math.

So I went to Fort Sill and had a ball with my friend Jimmy Snyder, drinking lots of cheap, 3.2 beer, and somehow passed the school. On weekends, I played in Lawton at a dreary, little nightclub in a place they called Boys' Town. Naturally, the scum that filled the club were attracted to me, and I to them, so I made lots of friends. I've never seen any of them since, but I learned a lot from the musicians there.

In January, they mustered all my class of National Guardsmen out of the U.S. Army, one day short of ever being able to receive benefits from military service, and sent us home.

A letter from a woman I had made friends with at the club in Lawton beat me to my mother's house by a couple of days. I had no sexual contact with this or any other woman during my short service term, but this letter read, in part, "I love you and will be glad to marry you the next time you're in Oklahoma." It was lying open on the night table in our bedroom when I arrived, and needless to say, Linda had read it.

I am certain this was the first seed of destruction on our long path to divorce sixteen years later. It has always been hard for me to remember this incident because of the pain attached to it, but there it is.

As a lesson for me in the rest of my life and for those unlucky, over-friendly slobs out there fixing to befriend a lonely lady at the bar, I will use a phrase from an already famous writer..."Who knows what evil lurks!"

An icy homecoming, but we made it through or around it, because there was no alternative.

I applied to the State of Arkansas for a job on the highway and got one, running the field laboratory. Not on the survey team like I thought! They taught me in one week all I'd needed to know about rocks, sand and concrete. I learned how to cook the moisture out of the mixture, weigh it, make bars out of it and test the stress it'd take by breaking it. And I got an orange station wagon to haul stuff around in. For this, they paid me two hundred dollars a month...ninety-nine dollars and ninety-nine cents every two weeks.

Linda and I rented a three-room house from Al Paudert right across the highway from my lab for fifty dollars a month. We had a small car note, and after paying utilities, we could go to a movie one pay period and out to eat the next. Period. We lived on canned goods and leftovers that both sets of parents brought over, and they kept Carla most of the time. I missed playing but had no way to do it.

And then fate intervened. I ran into Jim Climber, and he asked me if I'd like to start playing again on weekends. I was happy for the opportunity, and hell, we needed the five or ten bucks I'd get paid. So I was back before a live audience no matter how meager.

One day, Jim's drummer, Melvin Talbot, asked me to come over to Charles Heinz's house to rehearse and maybe play in his band. Charles had a pretty big regional hit followed by a very, big car wreck. He'd been out for awhile getting put back together so he could return to his career. Charles liked both me and my playing and wanted me in his band.

But that same day, two strangers came to Melvin's house where we were rehearsing and pulled me aside. They were Terry Johnson and Ronnie "Angel" Stoots, and they said they played with a band called The Royal Spades. They said they really liked the way I played and wondered if I'd like to join their band.

"We're gonna play some SHIT, man," said Terry. "We already have a tenor and a bari. We just need you to fill it out."

I liked the way Terry talked, and Ronnie was really good looking. They wore their collars turned up in back, and I could tell they were "cool" guys. So I said I would and after apologizing to Melvin and Charlie, took off with them. It was the best decision of my life!

We went over to Terry's house, and there waiting to get under way was Steve Cropper on guitar, Duck Dunn on bass, Don Nix on baritone sax and Charles "Packy" Axton on tenor sax. Terry played drums, I was on trumpet and Ronnie Angel was lead singer.

After introductions and small talk, Terry sat down on his drum stool and counted off a tune we would play every time we got to perform, *Sack O' Woe,* by Cannonball Adderley, a standard jazz classic.

I didn't know any of their tunes, but it didn't take me long to catch on. And they liked the ones I knew, so we added them to the repertoire. They loved *Cherry Pink, Tennessee Waltz* and *Stardust.* We all had a learning experience, and all of us really loved the sound of three horns together. We could do a good rendering of almost all the R&B hits we loved so much from Little Richard, Fats Domino, Ray Charles, and Chuck Jackson! Ronnie sang his ass off, too. Don sang some songs and could dance. Steve Cropper played the damndest rock, rhythm and blues guitar you ever heard and would wind up pickin' his guitar behind his head and slung down low between his legs. The crowd ate it up! Ronnie and I clowned around and danced on stage. We'd do most anything to keep the crowd looking at us and laughing or dancing. Duck just shook his mighty red head and swung his new Fender bass around madly in time to the music. God, could he whomp it!

The first gig I played with them was at a Catholic School named Little Flower. I was the new guy and from over in West Memphis. They teased me about my shoes a lot, but I didn't mind! The kids loved us and hooted and clapped!

I did manage to get new shoes before the next gig though. It was at Billy Hill's Starlight Supper Club out the highway toward Millington Air Base, eight or ten miles north of Memphis.

It was a rainy night, and nobody showed up. But it was a good rehearsal anyway. Billy cooked us catfish and fries and gave us some beer, which he shouldn't have done. Nobody was of age.

Christmas came and the State of Arkansas, in traditional, government holiday spirit, laid off a bunch of highway workers including me!

Since we were already living in Al Paudert's rental house, he let me go back to work at the airfield, and that's the way we sustained life between gigs with the band.

I got up early, went down and opened up, turning on the fuel pumps and the unicom radio and pulling any planes from the hanger that were slated to fly that morning. I loved doing it, and I was happy. I knew something good was going to happen.

It went on for months like that, and it was getting harder and harder to be at the field at the crack of dawn. Al wasn't very happy about that.

Meanwhile, Packy's mother, Mrs. Estelle Axton, wanted the band to go into the studio and record an instrumental, so she booked a day. She owned half interest in Satellite Records and her brother, Jim Stewart, owned the other half. That's how we got in the studio in the first place, by decree of "Mom," as some of us called her. She was our benefactor, and the reason for my life in this business.

A man named Chips Moman was there at the studio, along with his friend Smoochie Smith, a country piano player and comedian. Chips came to work for Jim, because he was a great guitarist and understood more about rhythm and blues than Jim, who was a left-handed, country fiddler and banker by trade.

They had named the day that we were supposed to show up and record with Chips as the engineer and producer. We were fine with that. Hell, none of us knew any technical stuff anyway.

We sauntered in one at a time, and there was Smoochie at the piano with a lick he and Chips were working on. They were trying to make an instrumental out of it, and that's no easy trick. The only reason they wanted one was because instrumentals were popular at the time, what with the success of Bill Black Combo's *White Silver Sands*, Bill Justice's *Raunchy* and Ace Cannon's *Cotton Fields Back Home.*

We were all helping as much as we could with Chips conducting or instructing. Terry had to attend his senior high school classes after the first day, and Duck said he was going fishing with his dad. A black tenor player who taught band in West Memphis, Gilbert Caple, came to bolster up the horns, and he brought a drummer named Curtis Green. Floyd Newman, a gifted, black bari-sax player who was a little older and a lot more experienced came and took Don Nix's place. Lewis Steinberg, the bass player who was later on *Green Onions*, came and took Duck's place. Chips decided the song didn't need a guitar after all, and that's why there isn't one on it. Floyd provided that quirky and comical voice that said, "Oh, last night," on the record. Packy took some shots at the solo and didn't satisfy anyone, so Gilbert did one...then another. The recording went on for about a week, as I remember, and the only constants were Chips, Smoochie, Packy and me. Everything else was swirling around us. People were coming and going!

Confused enough?

It ain't over yet!

As I remember, Ms. Axton and Ronnie Stoots were the ones who said we should change our name because of the possible racial slur. Ronnie thought the French word, Marquis, would be good, since we were already the "royal." I do NOT remember who actually came up with, The Mar-Keys, but I think it was Ms. Axton. She was very bright, HIP, as we would have said. She said something about the piano keys from the organ that did the riff in the song, and she was the one smart enough to reduce it down to Mar-Keys.

Like I said, that's what I remember from way back yonder. There are lots of versions from people with all kinds of agendas, but like I say, "I was there."

Ms. Axton was the person who believed in *Last Night*. She got so mad at her brother for NOT believing that she bet him one hundred dollars it was a hit. His face got red, and he shouted, "Okay then!" and slapped the wall where he was standing.

I think he really hated us, especially Estelle's husband, Everett, who showed up everyday after work at the Kellogg plant and stood around out front of the studio, drinking Busch beer from quart bottles in brown paper bags. He was drunk by six or so, and since it was his house Estelle had borrowed the money on to get the studio in the first place, he would begin to pontificate. Jim thought it was in bad taste and tried to shoo Everett off. That infuriated Packy, and he and Jim would verbally abuse each other. Ms. Axton would have to get between them.

It was in this climate that our record came out. And it was to my joyous surprise when they told me I would be listed as an artist, as opposed to Chips, Smoochie, Packy and Floyd who would be listed as writers. I didn't know the money would be so vastly different over a lifetime. And even if I had, I don't know how I would have changed things. I was just young and wet behind the ears, and probably couldn't have spelled publishing if you had asked me to. "I'm an artist," I proudly exclaimed to my parents when I got home. And so I was. It was a small piece of pie, but it was the key to my future.

It's here where a disk jockey named Dewey Phillips comes into the story. He had a show called, "Red Hot & Blue," and if you didn't listen to it you weren't hip. He was the first guy to play Elvis Presley. He was "the guy." Period. When he heard *Last Night*, he went nuts. He played it over and over.

The first time I heard it on the radio I was on my way back to West Memphis in my '51 Plymouth after being at the studio for some reason, probably just hanging out and playing hooky from the airport.

There are a few things in this world that truly classify as FIRST TIME THINGS, and let me tell you, hearing yourself on the radio for the first time is almost at the top of the list!! I was a teenager, and suddenly, Dewey Phillips was rasping out in that nutso voice of his, "Here are the Mar-Keys, guys and gals, with their brand new smash hit, *Last Night*!! He played it three times in a row, and each time my heart almost stopped. I wanted to pinch myself to see if I was dreaming. "And you heard it for the very first time right here on good old WHBQ! Fifty-six on your radio dial! RED HOT & BLUE!"

MY GOD! I felt the warm glow of religious passion, sexual delight and disbelief well up in me all at the same time. Surely I was hallucinating! I was speechless. I had no idea of what this meant or could mean, but I did know I just heard our record on the radio. In every two bar break, Dewey had some remark about Pabst Blue Ribbon Beer, and he was so excited he was babbling.

Soon Dewey started hanging out at the studio, and we got to know this genuine, twenty-four karat character. If it wasn't for him, Stax Records might not have jumped into the world spotlight so fast. And he never got proper credit, so I'm giving it now.

We started giging fast and furious all over town, and the record went to the top of the charts in Memphis.

Al Paudert and crew at the airport just shook their heads and grinned when I told them, but soon they were hearing the song on the radio, too, and started getting excited for me. When I couldn't get to work, they now understood and wished me well.

Linda and Mom and Dad were all happy if a little apprehensive about what the future might hold but never said discouraging words.

Memphis had around a million people, and we sold three thousand copies locally. Three percent of the market, which was considered saturation at that time. Jerry Wexler at Atlantic Records in New York heard about it. He wanted to promote it worldwide and leased the master recording from Jim.

The record began climbing the national charts, and we went into the studio and started work on the follow-up album. I was on full charge constantly. We all were.

We took promotional photos next. The only bummer was that Ronnie was not included, because we were an instrumental band. The studio got us a Chevrolet Greenbriar (we had to pay the notes) and new suits from Lansky's on Beale Street, where Elvis bought his clothes. Ray Brown, " The Round Mound of Brown Sounds," was going to take over booking. I mean a BOOKING AGENT!!

Somewhere the door had opened, and sunshine was pouring in on me. I didn't know that in stepping through, I would take on the sun AND the rain, and I didn't care. I was whistling. I was happy. I was ready. I had waved my Magic Wand for the very first time! And what began to happen next, could have only taken place "IN MY WILDEST DREAMS."

Here Come The Mar-Keys

In 1961, one of our first major coups was a booking on the fabulous Everly Brothers Tour. *Last Night* was the number two R&B song and the number three pop song. We were excited! We were hot! And Dad was worried.

However, as luck would have it, Charlie Rich was a friend of my Dad's from many afternoons spent at Pat's Lounge in West Memphis. He too, would be on the trip. So Dad took some comfort in the fact that Charlie could keep an eye on me. After all, Charlie was ten years older than me and had been on these tours before.

But I doubt one like this. It was the rock and roll tour to end all rock and roll tours!

Everybody was on this thing...The Everly Brothers, Freddie Cannon, Mark Dinning, Bobby Vee, Jerry Lee Lewis, Tex Ritter, Faron Young, Charlie Rich, Bobby Vinton, Jack Scott, The Mar-Keys and more.

We joined up for the southern leg of the tour through Birmingham, Montgomery and the biggest concert in rock & roll history up to that point, the Gator Bowl in Jacksonville, Florida.

We arrived at the motel in Birmingham in the pouring rain and went to the front desk to check in. There was a man on crutches behind the desk in a very bad mood. He loudly dropped the switchboard headset and drug himself over to face us.

"You must be the group from Memphis," he said, "Holy Mother, I can't even get a minute to call the law!"

He checked us in and gave us our keys. It turned out we were on the third floor of the little motel built around a swimming pool. All this poor man's trouble seemed to be coming from the second and third floors where the tour was lodged.

"I wish y'all would go up there and find out who it was that jumped from the second floor railing naked," he sighed. "Somebody's gonna get killed if I don't get that stopped."

We all dutifully stared out the window behind him at the second floor and just then, a naked figure with a flaming newspaper rolled up and stuck between his butt cheeks came dashing from a room and dove head first through the pouring rain into the pool below.

Don Nix, Steve Cropper, Packy Axton, Duck Dunn,Terry Johnson, Smoochie Smith, and Wayne (not pictured) Ronnie "Angel" Stoots

"There goes that son-of-a-bitch AGAIN!" the crippled man shrieked. He pulled himself back over to the switchboard and dialed a number we thought was surely the police.

I picked up my room key, bag and horn case and went out the door to the driveway, then up the wrought iron stairs to my room. God, I thought, what's going on? But I was grinning like a kid just arriving at the party. There was a dripping man going up the stairs across from me. I couldn't tell who it was because of the streaming, black hair stuck to his face. He'd lost the flaming paper now, and his privates flapped back and forth in front of him in a most comical manner. Comical to everyone except the cripple who I could still hear screaming at the top of his lungs from the office I'd just left.

"You son-of-a bitch!"

I dropped my bags off in my designated room and hurried back out to see what was happening. The mystery man was gone, so I followed the big, wet splotches down the concrete until they curved under a door. I stopped and knocked. By the look on Faron Young's face when he opened it up, I think he was fully expecting the cops. His eyes were round, and he held a white towel in front of him. "Yes," he said, with an exaggerated look of innocence on his face. "May I help you?"

"I'm Wayne Jackson."

From inside the room I heard Charlie Rich say, "Let him in, it's family," as he fell back on the bed laughing.

They let me in and then locked the door and closed the curtains. Everyone began "shushing" each other. I felt like I'd been allowed into the den of the mountain king, but I was scared of being arrested with this wild bunch.

I needn't have worried. This was a big event for Birmingham. The city was counting on a show the following day to fill all the hotels in town and not disappoint Coca-Cola who was sponsoring the whole thing. The little man at the desk wasn't going to call the police to come out unless someone got killed.

Faron Young had one of the nastiest mouths on any human I had met. He was using it nonstop when I came in the room and nonstop when I left. He pulled a girl's dress up and shouted something awful. She screamed, and he turned red-faced laughing.

Charlie tried to laugh, but I just sat in my chair near the bathroom and stared at Mr. *Hello Walls* as he destroyed my opinion of him. I could hardly wait to get out of there, and I felt sorry for Charlie who was just lying there getting drunk. I wondered what he would have to say to my Dad about this.

Finally, night came, and it was time to go to the theater. There was no rehearsal. You just told the stagehands how many mikes were needed, and they set them up. In our case, we all played around one mike while Ronnie sang on another, but we needed an extra when Don and I cavorted around on stage.

The theater was standing room only. There were so many acts that they had us waiting out in the alley in the drizzle under umbrellas.

Since we had a current hit going, we were near the end of the show. And because we were so young, some of the other acts like Bobby Vee didn't have too much to say. "Who gives a damn," was our battle cry, and we meant it. We were triumphant that night. The crowd went wild for us. Then they went wild for Jerry Lee and Charlie, too, so the boys from Memphis were doing well.

The next day, we loaded up in buses and drove to Montgomery where we had the whole eleventh floor of the grand, old hotel downtown. It was blocked, so no one could get up there without a pass. Of course, all the entertainers gave every pretty girl they saw a pass.

The show that night was a wonderful evening of hardwood floors, cheering crowds and camaraderie on the side of the arena floor where we performed. Again, the boys from Memphis were a smash.

After the show that night, we were all on the eleventh floor partying and congratulating each other. It was a time of making lifelong friends, exchanging phone numbers and honing contacts for future use in the business. I was having a ball talking to Mark Dinning who had a very pretty airline stewardess on his lap, when suddenly the door burst open. A big guy strode over and broke Mark's nose with one straight punch to the face while jerking the girl up from his lap at the same time. Nobody said a word as the guy dragged his wailing girlfriend out to the elevator. Mark put his hands over his face as the blood gushed through his fingers. He groaned and begged for a doctor. I got a towel from the bathroom to hold on his face and went with him to the hospital where they bandaged him up. After that I called him "Teeth," because he had a huge smile, which was all you could see under his bandages.

Late that night, I sat alone in the hotel coffee shop looking at the menu. My eyes were red and gritty, and nothing looked good. Then Tex Ritter walked in, spied me sitting all alone and ambled over. Someone told me he was running for governor of the state of Texas, so I couldn't believe he was going to sit down across the table from me. He was a big man with a booming laugh.

"Whatsa matta, boy? You look a little bushed. I know just what'll fix you right up!" And he ordered breakfast for me. The same one he was getting. My eyes bugged as the food came out, and I ate all I could. After thanking Tex, I excused myself to get a little rest before wake up call.

"Put some drops in them eyes, boy," was his parting remark.

"Yes, sir, Mr. Ritter."

The next day we all flew to Jacksonville on an American Airlines prop job. The plane was a riot of laughing, joke telling and groaning, especially when I discovered I'd left my trumpet at the airport. The stewardess asked me what was wrong and took pity. She had the captain call back for someone to go find it and put it on the next plane to Jacksonville. Then it would be brought to the hotel. I was embarrassed, but I survived.

Before we landed, every stewardess and every other female on the plane was invited to the concert and begged to come backstage after for a "little celebration." My head was swimming. What if Linda found out how much fun this all was? Would she make me quit? I forged ahead as if this were the only night left before somebody pulled the plug and said, “Sorry kid, there’s been a mistake, you’ll have to go home now.”

We arrived at the hotel just in time to go to our rooms, get out the Lansky Brothers’ suit bags containing our new uniforms, clean up a little and go back to the lobby to catch the shuttle over to the Gator Bowl. It was hot as blue blazes that afternoon when we arrived, and there were only a few small house trailers for dressing rooms, not enough for everyone. Being too shy to demand one, we stood around in the shade of the huge stage and watched the goings on. It was the best place to be anyway. We just ate up the excitement in the air and began feeling the adrenaline build for our time on the big stage in front of fifty-two thousand people! The Gator Bowl was packed!

There was actually a barricade between us and the crowd, as if someone would need protecting, and cops lined up to see that nobody came through. We thrilled at the thought of being “protected” from adoring fans! It was too wild, like a dream.

Coke-a-Cola was sponsoring the concert, and they gave away fifty-two thousand Cokes and fifty-two thousand hot dogs. You could buy beer and other refreshments, too. Everybody had at least two free hot dogs and a big cup of Coke or beer.

Local bands had been playing since the gates opened at noon. But now the sun was setting, and the real show was about to start. Dignitaries including disk jockeys and politicians lined the stage, each waiting to deliver his or her message to the crowd. It went on for thirty minutes, but soon irreverence reared its head in the crowd. They were ready to party.

“Okay! Okay!” shouted the mayor. “Y’all have a good time here in Greater Jacksonville, and y’all come back! Ya’ hear?”

The disk jockey that was the MC waved the mayor off and cleared his throat.

“WELL, IT’S TIME TO ROCK AND ROLL! THIS IS THE BIGGEST CAVALCADE OF STARS THE WORLD HAS EVER SEEN,” he shouted. “AND TO GET THINGS STARTED WITH A BANG, HERE’S THE GREAT SHOWMAN HIMSELF, FREDDIE CANNON!”

The crowd roared.

Freddie did his damndest and went over great. Since he was the first act, he did about forty minutes.

Then out came a big favorite, *Teen Angel*, himself, Mark Dinning, bandages and all. It confirmed what the crowd already suspected...the tour was just a raging party on the road, moving from town to town, complete with drunken brawls. They went wild. I noticed some of the other Mar-Keys had already changed into their suits, so I hurried over to the trailer where they were congregated and waited my turn to go in. The suits Lansky sold us were black, peg leg pants and double-breasted coats with white velvet on the pocket flaps and around the back of the collar. Bands were wearing uniforms then, and we were the sharpest, looking a little like Nazi tank drivers.

We were starting to sweat more freely what with the suits, the afternoon heat and the fact that our time was coming. It was running down my legs.

Charlie Rich went on and began crooning to the audience. He was so good-looking that the girls screamed and the guys gawked. He had them going pretty good, and when he got into *Mohair Sam*, they were jumping up and down. He finished to thunderous applause and screaming.

Then it was Jerry Lee's turn. The MC got the crowd all steamed up, clapping his hands over his head and beginning a chant, "JERRY LEE, JERRY LEE, JERRY LEE!"

But no Jerry Lee.

The MC walked over to the side of the stage and looked behind the backdrop curtain. The chant began to die down, so he grabbed the mike and began again, "JERRY LEE, JERRY LEE!"

Jerry was in his trailer, miffed by the crowd's reaction to Charlie. His band was standing around the trailer door begging him to come on, but he was having a hard time with inspiration under the circumstances.

"Man, you're gonna loose these people," said Hawk, the drummer.

In the distance, the chant was dying out again. Rock and roll crowds are funny.

The promoter was standing there, too. "Come on now, Killer, it's time to go out there and tear 'em up!" he said.

Slowly, the great Jerry Lee rose from his dressing table, combed his hair one last time and descended the steps of the trailer. His band went up the backstairs of the stage, got in position and started Jerry's music while the MC ranted and raved about " THE KILLER."

"HERE HE COMES, HERE HE COMES!!"

Jerry is a genius at this stuff. The crowd was frothing at the mouth when he finally mounted the stage and stood poised over the piano, ready to attack!

He lifted one long, skinny leg over the piano bench, reached one long, skinny arm down and tickled the ivories a little. The crowd bellowed and surged forward. They were ready for Jerry Lee. The Killer!

Then fate took over, and time stood still for an instant.

A hot dog lifted up from the crowd, and arching forward as it passed through the beam of the spotlight, instantly became the star of the show. It landed with a splat on the strings of Jerry's opened Baldwin concert grand.

The hush spread like a smoke ring. The crowd waited breathlessly for his reaction.

Jerry stared at the hot dog and then back at the crowd. He cut his eyes back at the hot dog, and a tremble went through him. The band still played his music, and after ten seconds or so, Jerry reached into his piano and gingerly picked up the hot dog. For a moment, it looked as if he might take a bite out of it. Instead, a look of rage swept across his face. He turned and threw it back at the audience. The crowd noise subsided for an instant, and then...

It rained hot dogs. It rained and rained hot dogs.

The people were shrieking with delight.

Everybody had three or four hot dogs lined up their arm and a pint of beer, and they'd been drinking all afternoon.

For awhile, Jerry picked up hot dogs and threw them back as the band ducked and attempted to keep playing. They were splattered head to toe with mustard and relish. Dogs were on the drums, and Hawk whacked away on them to a rock and roll beat. It went on and on. Then Jerry's plan to have a little fun with a bizarre incident took a turn. The floor was greasy with dogs, and the MC came squishing out in them to try to quiet the crowd and get the show back on track. But they had to get Jerry and the band off stage to get it stopped.

They promised the crowd that Jerry Lee would come back toward the end of the show. Everybody seemed to silently agree that a pause was needed to re-establish order. In the meantime, a crew came out and tried to clean the goo off the stage.

It was our turn. We were standing over to the side, ready, if not a little nervous, and in awe of what had just happened. Jerry Lee had pulled it off again! How do you follow THAT?

But we were game and after a huge build up, we trooped out on the stage and began our show.

The crowd looked like a sea of malignant, red eyes and sunburned faces, drunk on beer and still carrying more hot dogs than they were going to eat. We did great except for slipping around in the slime left over from Jerry Lee's disaster. Then we came to our closer and only hit, *Last Night*.

The crowd loved it, and I guess just couldn't help showing their appreciation by launching a few hot dogs our way. One hit the end of my trumpet and went up my bell choking off the sound. I shook it out and continued playing and stepping. Then Don Nix did it to us. He bent down, picked up a dog and threw it at the crowd. They were still game, and it rained hot dogs again, one going down Packy's sax bell. He pulled it out and threw it back. We were laughing like crazy, and since it was time for us to get off anyway, it wasn't too bad. We just hammed it up and waved goodbye naturally as we ran off through the ooze and falling buns.

Our uniforms needed a good cleaning, but we had fun and a taste of the big time. Plus, I had made some long-lasting friendships and gotten to know Charlie Rich and Faron Young very well.

We went back home, paid the bills and enjoyed running around town telling the tale of Jacksonville to all our friends, especially to the unbelieving people at the studio.

"Is that the way white folks act when they havin' fun?" they laughed. "Damn!"

We were the hottest band in town, and gigs continued to pour in. Even Elvis was a fan of ours! One night we were playing The Rainbow Terrace Room at Clearpool Lake, a building next to the largest public swimming pool in Memphis, and the King himself came out to hear us in his mouthwatering, pink Cadillac with a couple of his gang, Charlie Hodge and "Chief." Since he wouldn't come in, he parked behind the club near the loading ramp to listen. During the break, we all congregated near the big round fan that drew smoke and stale beer fumes from the club out into the humid Memphis night.

Ronnie Stoots and Elvis were pretty tight. They were hammering away about who knows what, girls and rhythm & blues included. Don was picking a fight with Packy while Terry, Steve, Duck and I discussed our wives and young children. Everyone was drinking and smoking except Elvis and Ronnie

Packy Axton, "Duck" Dunn, Wayne, Terry Johnson, Don Nix, Steve Cropper, "Smoochie" Smith, (not pictured) Ronnie "Angel" Stoots

and of course, Elvis' crew.

"If they don't put our picture on the next album cover," said Don, "I'll tell you what I'm gonna do! I'm goin' in that little chicken shit's office and kick his little red ass! That's what I'm gonna do!"

"You're not either," said Packy, and sloshed Thunderbird wine on Don's new Beatle boots. "Their selling this record to BLACK people and that would just screw everything up!"

"Well how about them BLACK people seeing our WHITE faces every time we go out to play, big boy, how about THAT?!"

Don was getting his usual tight, white lip expression he got when he talked about the band's publicity. The record company's "no pictures" policy was making all of us uncomfortable, because nobody realized we were white until we pulled up at a gig. Many times promoters got the jitters, and the crowd got mad, at least until The Mar-Keys started playing. The music would settle everyone down. Black crowds couldn't believe their ears. This bunch of white boys were FUNKY! Nervous to be sure, but FUNKY! We didn't know it then, but we were the real, original Blues Brothers.

"Man, I really dig those horns," Elvis was saying. "They give the band a real kick! Maybe someday you guys can come out on the road with me and put the shine on the trio."

Ronnie had his fists clinched down by his side. He could see himself being left out again. "That would be cool man. I could go along and be the opening act," he said.

"Yeah, man," Elvis replied, looking down and nodding his head. "Yeah." He had nothing to do with who got the opening spot in his show, but he liked Ronnie and his singing and hated to make him feel like he wouldn't help a friend. "I'll talk to the Colonel about it and let you know. When I get back to Memphis this next time, maybe we can work something out."

This talk had everyone excited, and we all began talking at once. We'd been at Ray Brown's National Artists Attractions about a year and had backed up everyone on his roster, so we had a little confidence in our ability. The volume rose until Packy's voice came crashing through. "We've got a twelve day tour of Texas booked before we can do anything," he screeched.

"Yeah, Packy, but damn man, Elvis!" said Terry. It summed up how everyone felt.

"We've got a contract," said Packy.

We all snuck looks over to Elvis who was grinning that catlike grin, knowing he had caused a row and enjoying the moment.

He put his hand on Packy's shoulder and said, "Don't worry about it man. It'll all work out," and opened the door to heaven, sliding onto the soft, white, bench style, leather seat on the driver's side. "Y'all go on back in there and knock me out again! Ain't it about time for the last set?" He had just unwrapped a cigar and stuck it in his mouth. It was a signal, and his two friends got in the car with him, Charlie in the front seat and Chief in the back.

"See ya, E," Steve said, and we all jumped for the back door to the stage. We got on the bandstand and began playing with real fire hoping to deeper snag "the big one." I guess he liked it. Sometime in the middle of the third song, we heard the tires throw gravel and squeal a little as that most sacred of all cars slid from the parking lot, out onto Highway 78 heading back toward Memphis.

That kind of thing went on a lot in'61.

But a soreness soon began to develop between those of us who had actually played on *Last Night* being designated either "artist" or "writer" and those who did not get a first royalty check. Don, Terry and Ronnie were left out entirely, but I remember the glow of holding a check for twenty-five hundred dollars in my hand that was made out to me! That was a lot of money at the time. Linda and I bought a yellow and white 1957 Ford Fairlane 500 Coupe and rented a house in Memphis at one hundred and fifty dollars a month. Things were looking good!

For the first time in my life, there was more money in the bank than was needed that month, not much, but a few months worth. It was a lot to me.

It felt good. It was freedom.

However, not everyone shared my jubilation. Don was sullen. Terry began talking of college in the fall. Ronnie didn't have much to say either. I didn't blame them, but I didn't offer them any of my royalties either. And I couldn't imagine the party ending so soon.

The Mar-Keys continued touring, drinking, laughing and fighting across the South after that. We put out a record called, *Bush Bash*, which made it up the charts for awhile giving everyone a better outlook.

We even did a short tour in Arkansas, booked again by Ray Brown. One of the gigs was at a drive-in movie in Newport, and we played on top of the concession stand. Imagine trying to get the drums not to slide off the back, because it definitely had a downward tilt! The front line had to play leaning forward, and you couldn't turn the mike loose or it would fall over backwards and roll off. After each song, there would be some horn tooting and headlight flashing, because the music was being pumped into the cars via the window speaker boxes, just like the movie sound. And when we played our big hit, *Last Night*, the audience of cars went nuts, blowing their horns like the devil was after them and flashing their lights like crazy. Some were even slamming the doors and screaming into the night. We went over really big, but getting down off that roof on the skinny ladder they provided was not as easy as going up. The popcorn smelled good though, and they gave us all a bag before we left.

The next night was actually in a club.The toilet in the men's room didn't flush, because it was just a trough that ran through a wall and out into the cotton patch. But it was a step up.

And then one day, after he and Packy had a big fight over who was the boss, Steve Cropper quit the band. He said he was going back to college, but he was really staying home on a deal he made with Jim Stewart. It was the beginning of a slow but certain unraveling. Steve enjoyed having fun, but he was no-nonsense at the same time. I liked that, because it made it easier for me to justify going to play. I'd say, "Steve this and Steve that, and everything's gonna be all right," to Mama and Linda.

After he left, Charlie Freeman took his place and though he out-played Steve, solo wise, he was a drug head. The Fifties had just gone past, when the word pot, let alone heroin, sent people running for cover. I was a naive kid from Arkansas who had just found out about diet pills and booze, and not much about that. But Charlie's intention in life was to get high. Which he did, until it killed him at the age of thirty.

We were all out every night sitting in, even if we weren't getting paid. After all, we were The Mar-Keys, loving the attention we got and the perks of young stardom, like everybody wanting to buy you drinks and the girls putting their hands all over you.

Linda was concerned with raising Carla. I never really knew how she felt about all this, because I never asked. I don't know what I would have done if she'd asked me to stop. I know she hurt a lot, but since she was so quiet, it was easy to over look. Carla was a self-sufficient kid from the start, and I thought I was giving her enough attention when I hugged her and waved goodbye as she rode off with her grandparents. Hell, we were teenagers... what did we know about parenting? What did we know about anything?

All the wives hurt a lot and some hurt more loudly than others.

But while on the road, we were free, forever running afoul of the wives, our agent, girlfriends, club owners, chicks, the cops, the parents and life in general.

Like the time we were on the loose in Texas.

The white 1961 Chevy Greenbriar with "Here Come The Mar-Keys" painted on the side in big, red letters continued south over U.S. 41 through Texas toward the first engagement of a fourteen day tour that was to start in Houston.

The only odd thing was that all the other traffic was headed north. ALL of it.

There were people camped on the side of the road, and every motel was full. We turned on the radio and found the weather station, along with the reason for the exodus north. We were headed straight into the watery teeth of Hurricane Carla, the biggest storm in fifty years. Houston was shut down tight.

Duck couldn't swim and was nervous. "Will it flood everything?"

There was starting to be no traffic at all and as we drove through Liberty, Texas, we decided to get a room, pulling into the Sunshine Motel.

"Sure I got a room," the old woman croaked and spit through her laughter. "Y'all look like you're lost or something," she said, pointing out to the empty parking lot. "Take your choice. Ain't nobody fool enough to be this close, I don't reckon." She was nearly toothless.

"When's this thing supposed to come through?" Don asked. He held his umbrella under his arm as though that might protect him from the coming storm.

"It'll hit tonight," the old lady said, staring straight into Don's eyes.

"Oh hell, well, let's hunker down." He put twenty dollars on the counter and promised to pay the rest of the fee the next morning. "We'll take those two in the corner over there."

We pulled all our things out of the Greenbriar and stuffed them into the rooms, along with ourselves.

All of a sudden, the sky was low, dark and angry. Everyone was looking around like, "What am I doing here?" I was excited, because I'd never thought I'd be in a storm like this. The wind had a different howl in it now, low and mournful, but heading for higher pitches. The trees waved crazily, and the little bus rocked with the wind gusts!

Then Hurricane Carla hit.

She smashed the Gulf coast with a Sunday punch and didn't pull back until the wee hours of the morning and then only for a short breather in the eye of the storm. We'd been cowering all night around the bed. Things were unearthly quiet, and the stars came out up high above the sagging, dripping palms.

"I wonder if there's anywhere to get something to eat," I said. "I think there's a diner down the road."

Duck had been on top of the bed all night quaking with fear of drowning. "A helluva' time you pick to get hungry," he growled. "I could die any minute." The parking lot was flooded all right.

"Who's got money anyway?" asked Smoochie. "I ain't got a nickel."

Nobody had money. We were depending on giging the first night.

"It doesn't matter anyway," said Ronnie in the brief quiet. "Here comes that roaring sound again." And the broad backside of Carla with the reverse winds did the rumba over the motel 'til past dawn.

With the passing of the deadly storm came a steady, but polite downpour, of the type that lasted awhile. There was enough money in the kitty to pay out of the motel and get some gas, but no more.

"Well, hell," said Ronnie, "let's get on with it."

We loaded up the Greenbriar and set off south again, not knowing what to expect...after all, we'd never seen a hurricane. Before leaving though, we pulled into a restaurant, and I talked the manager into giving us eight ham sandwiches, eight pieces of pie and eight cokes for the Benrus Sea-King watch my Daddy had given me for Christmas. We munched as we rode.

Galveston was in shambles as was all of the Gulf Coast. The Pier, where we were supposed to play, was a mass of twisted steel and splintered wood, held up by pylons and cables snaking through the wreckage like tentacles of an undersea monster. The debris stretched off down the beach and out into the lashing Gulf of Mexico.

"Well, hell," said Don after surveying the situation in awed silence for a few moments. He swung his umbrella around by the handle, "Here we are five hundred miles from home with no gig and no money! So what do you think now?"

He directed his attention to Charlie, the cool one.

"Who gives a damn?" said Charlie in his easy manner. "Call New York and tell them to send us some money. Tell them the bus broke."

Reservations had been made in advance of the tour, so before actually checking in at the Sea and Surf Motel, Don asked the Mexican behind the desk if he could use the telephone to make a collect call.

"Chure," he said and put the black rotary phone up on the counter.

Even though Packy was designated "leader" of the band, Don often spoke to higher-ups, because Packy was drunk and disrespectful.

He dialed Jerry Wexler's office number at Atlantic Records in New York City and soon got Jerry on the phone. "That's what I said, collect." He turned and leaned his back against the counter, so we could all see his face. "We're sittin' down here in Texas without a cent, and the bus broke down, Jerry, so yeah, collect. (Pause) OUR bus, that's whose! Gee whiz, did you ever see a hurricane? I think the water screwed up the engine or something. It was blowin' like hell. Now the thing's sputtering and won't go, and the mechanic at the Gulf Station says it needs six hundred dollars worth of work. We need expense money. So how much money's in the fund?" (Long Pause) Don smiled.

Three hours later, eight hundred dollars showed up at Western Union, and six hours after that, we showed up in Villa Cuana, Mexico.

A bottle of five-milligram dexamil tablets was five dollars, a quart of rum was four dollars and the girls were plentiful. It was a party like none of us had experienced, and it went on for two days. On the third day, everybody was pretty tired and disgusted and scared our wives would find out. Somehow we made it back to our hotel room on the State side of the border and called our agent to see what had happened. We all crowded into the Lysol-stinking, little room and listened to Don on the phone with our agent.

"They want us when?"

There was a pause, and Don's eyes got bigger and bigger. He cupped his hands over the mouthpiece and looked at us all.

"They want us on the Brook Benton tour starting Friday. And this is Wednesday," he gulped. "What do y'all think?"

"What do you mean?" said Packy. "Of course we want it!"

"But we pick it up in Myrtle Beach, South Carolina, eighteen hundred miles from here," he said, "day after tomorrow!"

"Damn," said Duck. "We'd better load up and hit it." He took a small vial from his shirt pocket and emptied four, green, heart-shaped pills into his mouth and washed them down with a glass of warm tap water. "I'm driving," he announced and stalked out to the van.

It was a long drive to the East Coast, but Duck did it all. The rest of us just grumbled and napped.

When we reached the field house in Myrtle Beach, it was almost show time, and we found out that Brook Benton's band hadn't shown up. They wanted us to back up everybody. We did our best, and it was only a small disaster. Small...yeah...but still a disaster.

We got back home irked with show business and ourselves in general. Everybody was sick of everything.

Up In Smoke

There were a string of difficulties with the band after that. A spiraling down through worse and worse clubs, fights and no-paying gigs. Duck left to go to work at Stax when Louie got into the bottle too much. I began selling vacuum cleaners, or should I say, a vacuum cleaner, to my mother. I knew it was over.

Tommy Cogbill, a bass player refugee from Chips Moman's band, and I got jobs at Electrolux together. We went through some training where they paid us seventy-five dollars a week. We then began banging aluminum tubing together up near poor people's heads and throwing dirt around their living rooms, until one day I threw a big bag of dirt down on this rural, black woman's floor. She said, "Now, how you gonna get dat up?"

"With this," I proclaimed, pulling out the old Electrolux.

"I can't wait to see dat," she cried, "I ain't got no 'lectricity!"

It was a good laugh all right, but that was that. She handed me a broom and a piece of cardboard, and I went to work.

Then Tommy and I tried some Lester Lannin big band gigs for awhile. They paid seventy-five dollars each, but we usually had to drive a long way and do hour after hour of fox trots and waltzes. Then we'd drink some and try to drive home, let's say from Huntsville, Alabama, to Memphis, to save hotel charges. We were young, but it was hard.

Tommy was the best guitar/bass player in the world, as he would soon prove at Chips' American Studio. As for me, I had lots of nerve. Most of those guys were out of New York City and could be as cold as ice to a kid from Memphis. But Tommy was so good, they let me ride and learn. When it was my turn to stand up, I did okay. I had that tone, so I didn't have to try to be flashy. I knew better. I just played it straight and pretty, and the people ate it up.

I loved Tommy and did 'til the day he died of a stroke in a Nashville hospital. We shared laughter and music, whiskey and long night rides, Electrolux and that bond musicians get when they're close that says,"We're great, we're havin' fun, and everything's gonna be all right." Exit smiling.

Tommy was working steadier than I was and though he tried to help, I was going down quicker and quicker. Then one day the phone rang at my house, and it was Charlie Hodge.

"Hey, Wayne," he said, "Ronnie Angel said you need a gig, and I got one.

You want it?"

"Yeah, yeah," I said, "but wait a minute, man, what's going on? How come you're callin' me?"

My breath caught. I thought for a minute he might be calling me for Elvis.

"Well, I'm workin' for Jimmy Wakley out in Las Vegas when Elvis is off the road. Jimmy told me to find him a trumpet player. You're it man, that is if you can sing. And Ronnie says you can sing. That right?"

"Sure, Charlie. What do I have to do?" I was wildly thinking of what to tell Linda.

Charlie Hodge was one of the legendary Foggy River Boys and had joined up with Elvis when they were in the service together in Germany. Now he was Elvis' right hand man on stage, but I had no idea he did separate gigs when he was off.

"Well, I'd like for you to come over to the house and audition. Tonight will be fine, if you can. I have to let Jimmy know something tomorrow."

His casual, too cool mention of the word "house," I knew, he meant the Presley mansion, "Graceland." I had never been there.

As I said earlier, I had auditioned for the Navy band in high school and failed. Mainly, because I had gotten very nervous, and I was getting very nervous now. I began dreading the coming trial with cold sweat.

I agreed to show up at the mansion by seven o'clock. Charlie said the guard would let me in the gate if I would have my driver's license ready, and I was to drive around back and park. He would meet us at the backdoor, and yes, I could bring Linda along. That made it worse. I had a hang-up about playing in front of her that came straight out of my Id. It was terrible. I've never figured it out, unless it could be I was afraid some chick would like me and piss her off. I was a child and that was long ago, but the big knot in my stomach was real.

I dressed in my best slacks and white shirt with my new, dark sport coat, big silver cuff links and the inevitable Beatle boots.

Linda dressed all afternoon right up until time to go but wound up in black slacks and a sweater, of course. As we got out of the car, we furiously picked at ourselves and each other, trying to get all the lint off. I almost got to the door without my trumpet. Damn, I thought, this has got to stop. So I took a deep breath and knocked on the door.

Charlie appeared an eternity later, dinner napkin in hand, wiping his mouth and mumbling, "Y'all come on in. I'm just finishing up some supper. Go on in the living room and make yourselves comfortable. I'll be right there."

He was dressed up fit to kill. It looked like a party to me, but Charlie was dining alone. I would find out later that dressing up was his habit. Elvis liked that and thought it was classy. Charlie was a small, well-built man, kind of like me, and he looked good in his clothes.

Linda and I drifted dreamlike into the hallway and through the kitchen where Charlie was eating, then on into the formal dining room with its massive chandelier, mahogany dining table and china cabinet full of crystal, just like Ronnie had said. We made our way across the formal entrance hall and into the lavishly furnished living room with its custom made, mile-long, white couch and drapes that looked straight out of a movie set...Dracula maybe. Boy, they were purple. There was a white baby grand piano across from the couch, and I frantically wondered if it was here I would be required to audition. My mouth was dry, but when I glanced over at Linda, I felt better. She was the color of a corpse, and as cold. I took her by the elbow and guided her over to the pearly white, velvet couch and broke her legs so she could sit. She looked up at me, and I felt like saying goodbye. Then Charlie walked into the room and cleared his throat, "Ahemmm, well how are y'all doing? Sorry I was busy when you came in, but I see you made it on in here! Good," he laughed. "Well, get it out, and we'll play something. What do you like to play?"

"*St. Louis Blues*," I croaked and blew the spit from my horn down onto the royal blue carpet. Where was that butler with that mop? I wondered. I prayed for control.

"What key?"

"The original, concert F," I answered. "If that's okay."

"Sure," said Charlie, beginning a slow, pretty introduction.

I felt a wave of relief. I didn't have to start cold. I slid right in and played the first verse effortlessly. Out of the corner of my eye, I could see Charlie smiling. Second verse, I added a little obligato at the end, and he played lovely passing changes to the bridge. Gotcha. This is where I shine. And I did. The final chorus began, and Charlie sang the refrain, "St. Louis Woman, with all your diamond rings, lead a man around by her apron strings."

It was going great, and then I saw Linda's eyes and heard that second voice at the same time. Oh, God no. Linda was sliding down into the cushions of the couch as that golden voice slid into the harmony parts with Charlie. I was jamming with Elvis Presley! And it sounded great!

At the end of the refrain, Charlie finished with a flourish and an adjustment of the big, ruby ring on his pinkie finger.

"I wondered if you were going to come down when you heard that trumpet," said Charlie.

"Shoot, yeah," said Elvis in his nasal drawl. "I couldn't resist. Come on, man, I like that!"

"Hi Wayne," he said, remembering my name. "And who might this be?" His eyes were sparkling in his god-like face, and he flashed his legendary grin.

"That's my wife, Linda," I said. They shook hands, and Linda just nodded, turning several shades of pink at the same time but actually said, "Hi."

Elvis was dressed in blue jeans and a loose fitting denim shirt, white socks and penny loafers.

"Well, come on y'all, let's do some more," he said. And we started into *Sentimental Journey*, at Charlie's suggestion.

I was loosening up by then, so when Charlie looked at me and said, "Now, you sing the third part," I just did it. It flowed out of me like I was a stranger. Then when he said to do a solo, I did my thing with the melody, and Elvis sang the second harmony. I dared not look over at Linda. I thought she might be levitating. I knew I was.

When that was over, Elvis went straight into *The Old Rugged Cross*. I played the solo when it came around, just straight and easy, with Elvis humming along. I could see Charlie eating it up. Somehow I was over my fear and enjoying myself immensely. Linda was wearing a huge smile. We were in. Into just what, I didn't know, but into something. Better than those cotton fields back home.

"Do you know anymore of those good blues?" Elvis asked.

"I know the *Basin St. Blues*," I said, and told Charlie, "in the original key, B flat." I thought that sounded professional.

Charlie did the famous intro, and I kicked into the first verse right on time. Elvis smiled and said, "Yes sir," a couple of times. But otherwise, he just sat back and enjoyed the tune. So did I and was sorry when it was over.

"Well, Charlie," said Elvis, "what do you think? Can he handle the job?"

"You bet E, you bet!" said Charlie with a laugh. Seems like everybody was onto that little joke but me. I didn't care though.

"Well now, I wish I didn't have to go," said Elvis, "but I'm going out with the gang tonight to catch a flick."

He stuck out his hand to shake mine. "Good luck, man." Then he walked over to Linda, bent down and kissed her on top of the head. "Y'all be careful, now, you hear?"

He left the room letting his open hand slide along my shoulders as he passed behind me.

"Come back anytime, man, and be sure to bring that horn."

I nodded my head. "Sure Elvis, thanks."

Charlie told me what date he expected me to be at Jimmy Wakley's house in Los Angeles, what time rehearsal began, and that he thought the gig would pay one hundred and sixty-five dollars a week, just for the weeks we worked. But he also thought for sure, I would work a lot in L.A. in the off time. We shook hands, and he gave me some phone numbers where he could be reached.

So we traded in our '55 Pontiac for a '59 blue and white Rambler station wagon, loaded up everything we had including three-year-old Carla, and Don Nix, who had some reason to go there, and headed out.

Much to our chagrin and surprise, the Rambler burned one quart of oil every hundred miles, nearly as much as it did gas. Finally, in Oklahoma City, we stopped and bought a case and an opener. Then every two hundred miles, we'd stop, get out, raise the hood and without checking the stick, add two quarts. You could write your name in the oil slick collected on the back of the wagon, but I wrote "California or bust" in it. Linda was not amused, and Don took another sleeping pill. He didn't drive one mile of the trip. Instead, he tucked his long legs under himself, leaned over on a pillow and snored and complained.

Three days later, we arrived in L.A. and dropped Don off where he was going. He didn't even say goodbye, just "see ya," and walked out of our life. Then we checked into a motel for some much-needed rest. After paying for the room, we had eleven dollars and change left.

The next day, we found Folsom Boulevard and the Wakley's residence, after one hell of a small town, hick experience on the expressway. In all the Mar-Keys' travels, there had been nothing to prepare me for that!

We went in the low, white, California style house surrounded by palm trees. Mrs. Wakley was very cordial and took us to the kitchen where she offered us coffee and Coke. She brought out some cookies, too. Linda and I were just twenty years old. I still had pimples. So with three-year-old Carla sitting there between us, we looked like what we were, a bunch of babies from Arkansas.

We met Linda Wakley, the daughter, who had just had a number one record with *Yes, I'm Lonesome Tonight.* She was pudgy and distant and actually held her nose up in the air like we smelled funny or something. We never liked her much either, although she was about our age and later softened a bit.

Next, we met Johnny Wakley, the blond, overweight son of Jimmy. He was cute at first, but his cursing soon got old. It was evident that he and his mother went round and round about it. He said "son of a bitch" and "God damn" almost every other word. Sometimes Mrs. Wakley would snatch up a dinner napkin and try to slap him across the face, but it didn't help. She told us later that she made Johnny stand in front of a mirror and sing songs made up entirely of curse words, for hours on end, trying to break him of his obscene habit, but to no avail. Johnny went on tour with us and could sing pretty well, but I always wanted to hear those late night "standing before the mirror songs."

Soon, Charlie and the rest of the band showed up. Our star, Mr. Wakley, came in from somewhere in the house. They set up, plugged in and began to run over some songs such as, *Cimarron Roll On*, at a tempo I'd only dreamed of, along with *Love Song of the Waterfall*, and *Ramona*. I didn't play a note. I had no clue about this music.

"Well, son," said Jimmy, not unkindly, "don't you think you ought to join in?"

"Yes sir," I replied. "I just don't know any of these songs."

Hershel Witt, the great Oklahoma guitar player whom I'd spoken to briefly in the parking lot and who knew about The Mar-Keys, shifted his toothpick to the other side of his mouth and cleared his throat. "Why don't you play one of those blues y'all are so famous for down there in Memphis?"

"Yeah," said Wakley, "let's do that!"

So we played *St. Louis Blues*, and I could feel the tension in the room ease off. Charlie Hodge fanned himself.

"Now that's more like it," Jimmy laughed, putting his hand on my shoulder. "Maybe we can do something with that." They were all relieved that

I could actually play.

The next day at rehearsal, though, was a different story.

"I'm sorry, Wayne," he said, right in front of everyone. "I know y'all drove a long way out here, but I've got to have someone who can play a lot more with the band on my Western numbers than you can. So I'll do like the union says and give you your two weeks notice. You can make the trip to the Commercial Hotel in Elko, Nevada, with us and then that's that."

He wasn't being mean. It was just the truth. I didn't know how to work with the band, and I realized with a sinking heart what a jam I had gotten us into. We were broke and eighteen hundred miles from home. Worse still, with a three-year-old.

But that night a real miracle happened. About seven o'clock a smiling Hershel Witt showed up at our motel room door.

"Hey, Wayne, git' yore' trumpet and come on with me. We're goin' out pickin'."

We went to a little place in Bakersfield, and after the band had played a few tunes, he and I got up and played some blues. I know now he just wanted to check me out to see if I could really play before he invested any time in me. Well, I must have passed muster, because the next night he showed up at our motel room with his guitar, sat down and started telling and showing me how to play country western licks on the trumpet. One at a time, every night, I'd learn a new lick for Jimmy's songs. By the time we got to Elko, Nevada, I'd learned enough so that Jimmy said, "Well, I guess I'll keep you on for another two weeks."

And so it went for the next seven months. Hershel working with me in the room at night, and at the end of the next two weeks ole' Jimmy would say, "Well, I guess I'll keep you two more weeks." I was learning a lot, and the crowds loved my blues solos. So I did earn my keep. I sang some background, too. It was the most "learning" period of my life, and a lot of the learning was about life. It all came in handy.

Jimmy was a keno player and played from the stage during his show, which the house must have loved. A girl sauntered up to the stage every five minutes and showed Jimmy what he had lost or won. He would mark the tickets quickly and so on all night long. He played at breakfast and dinner, and if he ever made love to his wife, I'm sure the little ticket girl was present every five minutes.

The first night in Elko, though, Jimmy announced, "And now, here's our young twenty-year-old trumpet picker all the way from Memphis to play the *Beale Street Blues*." Well, that ended any thoughts I might have had about gambling. The guards wouldn't allow Linda and I out of the dressing room area, unless we had Carla with us. Then they'd goad us into letting her play the penny, electric slots, much to our chagrin. Even worse, she would win, to the guards delight! I'd hold her up, she'd drop in a penny and pull the arm, almost always getting at least five or ten or twenty-five pennies back. She'd wind up with a little bag of pennies, and everybody loved her. She was the star of our show.

Elko was a real cowboy town in the Sixties, complete with whorehouses, cowpokes and horses tied up at the hotel hitchin' post, just like the movies. You could see the range from anywhere in town, and big game hunters with elk or deer strapped across hoods of their pick-ups were at every turn.

There were Indians around, too. They hung out on the corners, in the darkened alleyways and at the edges of parking lots under street lamps. They were usually dirty looking and broke, not welcome in the casinos. When they were drunk, they were scary. One night when I had hours to kill before a show, some Indians I encountered on the sidewalk outside the hotel invited me up to the top of the mesa with them to have a bon-fire and stargaze. I went. Big mistake. Everything was okay for awhile, and then the Indians started drinking and dancing. They wanted me to dance, too, but I was embarrassed and nervous. They didn't care and started to get loud and angry.

So I told them about my Choctaw blood, sixteenth part. That didn't bother them, except then they really wanted me to dance. I couldn't drink either, I told them, as I refused the bottle, because I had to get back to work. They didn't seem to like or understand that. I was only minutes from begging, which would have gotten me killed, when someone finally took pity on me and said, "You better let us take you back to town."

I got in their pick-up truck and stared straight ahead, praying my way back to the hotel.

After that, I never went with the Indians again. It was years before I told anybody else I had Indian blood in me.

And finally one day, Jimmy fired me. I was tired of the drill anyway, so I thanked him for the opportunity to work with him and learn and said farewell.

Linda and Carla were with me on the way back to the motel that we were so in debt to when a cop pulled us over and asked to see my driver's license. He walked around the car looking us over real good, then came back to the driver's window and said, "Well, you've got Arkansas plates, a Tennessee driver's license and a California residence. You were speeding and made an illegal turn at that corner back there. Gee, I don't know where to start."

But he was smiling and asked how old Carla was. We told him, and he took off his hat and wiped brow. "Hell," he said, shaking his head, "this is going to take forever. Why don't you guys just go on back home and get some of this straightened out? That way if I stop you again, I won't have such a mess on my hands." We thanked him and said we'd do just that, but I thought I had an ace in the hole!

I had gone to the Palomino Club in Hollywood one night with Herschel to sit in. The band was knocked out, and I told the bandleader I needed a job. He hired me on the spot. I was saved!

Back at the motel, I excitedly told Linda I had a job, and we would be staying in California after all! I don't think she was too happy to hear it, but she didn't say anything.

The next day I went to the L.A. Musicians Union to tell them I had a job at the Palomino Club working six nights a week. The lady behind the desk said that was wonderful except that according to union law, I could work no more than two nights a week at any one job until I'd lived in the L.A. area for six months. She said it was to protect their long-standing members from people coming to town and taking their gigs.

"Well, how am I supposed to live if I can't work?" I protested. But the lady just shrugged and said, "That's the rules."

It was the last straw. Linda and I called home for some help to cash out of that godforsaken motel. We had just enough money for tacos and cokes, twice a day, all the way home. At three for a dollar taco stands, we all got one and split the coke. We used Mr. Christopher's credit card for gas and lots of oil.

Along the way, we stopped in Amarillo, Texas, to see Mona and Glendon Franks, some old friends who had moved there after joining the Air Force upon finishing high school. That's where I turned twenty-one. I went down to a beer joint with Glendon to buy a legal beer. I ordered and proudly put my driver's license on the counter, ready to tell the bartender it was November the 24th. The bartender never even looked at it.

The next day we took off again for Arkansas. I've wondered many times what the story of my life would have been had the lady at the L.A. local just shut up and stamped my card.

We arrived back in Earle, Arkansas, with three dollars and fifty cents, just about the same as we'd arrived in California with seven months before. But I had a major link of my education in place, and we were all well and happy.

However, I had a bad taste in my mouth for California that lasted many years. That is until I went back on a jet plane and was picked up by The Doobie Brothers' limousine.

Memphis Rocked

We decided to leave Carla out on the farm with her grandparents while we went the sixteen miles into West Memphis to live with my parents and find the next step in our lives. They were relieved to see us and readily agreed that we should stay with them, at least for now, while I looked for a job. Linda had finished her high school education right at my parent's kitchen table, and that's what they thought I should do, too.

I agreed with Dad that I should get a job around town at the case factory or someplace, but I couldn't resist calling Duck Dunn to ask what was going on with The Mar-Keys.

"We're playing the weekends at The 1600 Club on Union Avenue. Why don't you come out Thursday night and see how it goes? The lady that owns the place will love you. She might even hire you."

It was all I needed.

"I'll be there," I said. That Thursday night I dressed up, and out I went.

One hour of music later, I was hired. The pay was eleven dollars a night, and I gladly accepted.

It was a beer joint, typical of Memphis in the Sixties, dark with low ceilings and pungent with the odor of pinesol and cigarettes. The customers were usually friendly until at least eleven o'clock. After that, you could hide in the smallish kitchen between sets and sneak out the backdoor after work. Unless, of course, you had relatives in the house. Then it was hell all night.

During the four months I was there, the band only got in a fight with the crowd once.

It was a Friday night. We were in the middle of *Going to Kansas City* when a guy came up and started hollering at Packy to play something by Ace Cannon. Packy just stuck the bell of his tenor sax in the man's face and went BALK!

The man turned crimson, and his eyes bugged out. He reached for Packy but was stopped by the huge, metal encased, head of Duck's Fender bass as it struck him full in the face. He dropped like a sack of wet cement. It was a melee in front of the bandstand, filled with shouting, snatching hair and ripping clothes. Finally, the boss lady came over, and somehow got things settled down.

Like I said, I was there four months. One night Blue Baron, the maitre d' from Lil' Abner's Rebel Room, came by and after hearing me play for an hour called me over to his table.

"Hey, kid, how'd ya like to come to work for me?"

It was too much like show business! I said, "Yes."

Two weeks later, I started a stint at Lil' Abner's that would last two and a half years. After I had been there for awhile, Buster Arnold, the owner, called me aside and said, "You can play that trumpet kid, but can you dance? I want to keep these people excited the whole time they're here. And while we're at it, do you sing?"

I had always loved dancing and singing, and like I said before, this was like show business. I never stopped dancing after that. And I learned to love singing for my supper, which I've enjoyed ever since. I learned to sing all kinds of songs, many old ballads and fast tunes, too. They ranged from *I Left My Heart in San Francisco* to *Going to Kansas City*. You couldn't have dragged me away from the Rebel Room with a bulldozer.

And while I was there, I began a friendship with Robert Tally, the black piano player, that would last a lifetime. He would educate me and enrich my playing to a level of professionalism I had no idea existed for me.

"Tally," as he was affectionately called, had been a trumpet player in his youth. During World War II, he had written and arranged many Armed Forces Special Services shows all by himself and then turned to the piano after coming home to Memphis. He knew he could gig more on piano than trumpet.

When I came along, Tally knew he had someone to pass his stuff on to. He came to work early every day for two years to teach me new songs and how to solo, which I thought I already knew.

"You've learned to play the trumpet, Waynie, now throw all that away and just listen," he'd say.

Tally could lead a blind child through a field of broken glass with his passing changes, and I began to get it. I began to listen. Making up horn arrangements on the spot came naturally to me. I didn't know it then, but it was to be my signature forte.

In an interview years later, Tally said, "Wayne can hear grass growin'!" I've never had a better compliment.

By the time Tally was done with me, I knew all the great ballads and all

Wayne, during his time at the Rebel Room in the mid 60's

the pretty passing changes, too. He loved my sound and led me through solos until I could feel all the strains running through them. It really got the folks going, especially the ladies.

"Don't forget who's bringin' dem men in here, Waynie," Tally would admonish me. And I didn't.

Blue Baron taught me that, too.

Blue knew all his customers by name. As they came in the entrance to pay their five bucks, he'd be right there to grin and shake hands with the men and hug and kiss the ladies. It was not lost on me that we were keeping the place packed every night. Since I was a polite, social person anyway, I followed suit. Soon, I, too, knew hundreds of customers on a first name basis and what songs they preferred. There were other benefits to this, also. My drink glass was never empty, and the patrons often handed me tips for songs that the band was going to do anyway. I stuck some of those in my pocket as I knew other band members were doing. So hustling tips became part of my education. After all, I was only making about eighty dollars a week, and I had to take all of that home for the bills. If I wanted cigarettes and gasoline, I had to hustle!

So we had our regulars and then some not so regulars, like the one who arrived one cold, December night.

The cotton bolls from Earle, Arkansas, to the wide Mississippi were empty from two pickings except for a few sad, little, white wisps dangling.

The roads were empty of farm equipment, only the rich folk's cars were speeding to Memphis for some excitement at the Peabody or the clubs. But one car crossed the Delta that night unseen by family eyes or state police. It crossed the bridge over the Mississippi River and went on out Bellevue Boulevard 'til it came to Lil' Abner's where it found an empty spot near the "band only" entrance and slid right in. The occupant looked in the mirror and applied a fresh smear of lip-gloss, straightened her hair for the final time, opened the door and got out. She was very happy.

She could hear the music blaring from the bandstand inside, and excitement coursed through her teenaged bones like hot water.

My brother-in-law's eldest daughter, seventeen-year-old Vicky, had arrived.

We had just finished one of my specialty numbers, where I went to the back of the room, climbed up on some unsuspecting customer's table and played, *I Can't Get Started With You* back at the band, across the dancing heads of the crowd. We called this "Rebel Room Stereo," and it was very popular. I often got fifty dollars in cash stuffed in my coat pocket on my way back to the bandstand. It went into the pot and was split along with all the other tips at the end of the night.

As I got back to the bandstand area, I saw this pretty blonde come in the backdoor in a full-length fur and stand there looking at me. She was not smiling but smirking a weird little smirk. She seemed to be saying, "WELL! I'm here!"

It took me a minute to realize who she was, and when I did, I was stunned. I hugged her and offered her a seat in the first booth by the door. She took it, and I told the owner, Buster Arnold, in the second booth, who she was and that she would be there for a few minutes as my guest. He chomped down on his cigar but shook his gray head okay.

Charles "Tennessee" Turner had just arrived from his set at the Plantation Inn, a club on the eastern end of West Memphis famous for its blues band led by Willie Mitchell. Each night, Charles traversed the Memphis/Arkansas bridge twice, doing one set at the P.I. and then one set at Lil' Abner's. Then he'd repeat the process.

He would come with his woven, many-colored Easter Basket and sing in his fabulous, Irish tenor voice. He was the blackest man with the widest nose I've ever seen, and gay to boot, but he could open up those golden pipes and let you have it. Then he would quip with the crowd, "That makes tears come to my pretty blue eyes." They would rush up to the bandstand and fill his basket with dollar bills, not coins.

Vicky sat in her preferred seat while "Sissy Charles" did his magic. Then she eased over to the railing next to the bandstand and motioned for me to come over. I did and leaned into her lovely form.

"Uncle Wayne," she purred, "do you mind if I dance?"

I had no feeling about that. I just smiled over at Buster. He was looking at me with no expression on his face. It was a "gimme another scotch" look.

That's all.

So I said, "No, I don't mind sweetheart."

I figured some dude would walk over and ask the beautiful, young woman to dance.

And I asked Tennessee, "Would you mind doing *Rollin' On The River*?"

He rolled his eyes and looked over his shoulder at me. I knew I would pay.

"Well, okay," he hissed.

Ed Logan was playing sax that night, and I counted off the song at a good strong tempo, hoping to give Vicky every opportunity to snag a partner.

Da,Da,Da...Da,Da,DA...DaDADADA DADAD,DADAh...DAAAAA!

We were under way.

I looked back at the dance floor after giving my full attention to the intro of the song and lost my breath.

Vicky had moved to center floor right in front of Tennessee Turner and dropped her full-length fur to the floor around her feet! Underneath was a red, velvet costume that had shimmy, shimmy, white strings hanging down her legs and her bosoms...AND she had silver batons in both hands, which she began to twirl!

The floor was full of dancers, and I choked up. I couldn't speak even if I could have invented something to say. The dancers slowly ground to a halt, staring slack-jawed at the center attraction and trying to laugh or clap, they couldn't decide which. Vicky kicked her legs up high and did a high school cry. The place was frozen in time. Slow motion and all. I did manage a look at Buster, and his cigar was hanging down from a gaping hole. He couldn't have moved if he'd wanted to.

When the song ended a century later I couldn't speak and don't remember what happened after that.

I don't remember how Vicky got out of the place. I don't remember if there were fights or if anyone threw anything. I didn't get fired, and I'm glad of that.

I can't even remember if I told Linda the next morning.

So if you were of consenting age and lived in Memphis in the Sixties, you were in automatic attendance of possibly the biggest and longest party ever to be thrown in any town. And you never knew what was going to happen.

I, myself, buzzed all over, in and out of any place that had a band where I could sit in. Speed being as popular as it was, no one ran out of energy.

The music that had been and was being created in Memphis could be found everywhere in a variety of clubs, lounges and hotels, both black and white.

Charlie Rich haunted the downtown jazz clubs and posh hotel bars. Jerry Lee circled the city playing all night honkytonks out on Brooks Road and South Bellevue. The old Sun Records had closed down, but its rock-a-billy and rock and roll sound was everywhere. Then there was the rhythm and blues coming out of Stax and Hi, and the mixed bag coming out of Chips' place. So a variety of stars spilled over from the studios into the clubs at night. You never knew who would be down at the Thunderbird Lounge to sit in with Flash and the Board of Directors or over at Herbie O'Mell's, T.J.'s Club, to sit in with Ronnie Milsap. Maybe B.J. Thomas or King Curtis or Alex Chilton from The Box-Tops. At John Fry's, Ardent Studio, on Madison Avenue, there was a constant flow of international stars recording and hanging out across the street at Overton Square, Memphis' answer to Bourbon Street at that time. It was a natural hang out for the local musicians too, anxious to score a big session.

The Manhattan Club featured The Willie Mitchell Band and The Four Kings, a black, singin'-their-asses-off group, dressed in mohair suits and STEPPIN'! And my mentor, Gene "Bowlegs" Miller was over at The Rosewood Club, a converted theater in a black neighborhood. Before Martin Luther King got killed, white people could go most anywhere without a problem. But, one night I got backed down the hall by a drunk, black man with a for-real looking knife. After I was saved by a black disk jockey, Bowlegs told me it just wasn't worth it, although I was getting to play a lot there up to that point.

All the hotels had live bands and out on Brooks Road, there was the ever-popular Hernando's Hideaway that featured a "tea dance" from two until five in the afternoon. Never saw any "tea" there, although I saw many a tea dancer slip out the backdoor with somebody else's roomy. It was a real redneck joint just like The Volcano Club, a former church that couldn't make it with the Christians, so Charlie Foren helped it go nightclub. Ronnie Angel and I opened it for him.

"Jumpin" Gene Simmons of *Haunted House* fame rocked The Diplomat Club, and if he wasn't there with his Little Green Men, then Sam The Sham and The Pharaohs would be.

Over on Third Street, there was The Red Velvet Club where you'd find the likes of Ace Cannon and Bobby Woods, both of whom had regional hits on the Hi label. Reggie Young and Mike Leech got their start there, too. That was a wild place. Ace would get drunk and climb the oak tree in the parking lot, refusing to come down until the police came with the dogs. Sometimes his father would join him, and the hollering would go on for an hour.

Clifford Curries' Tropicana was where the big blues acts performed. Now THAT was a fun joint! If Johnnie Taylor was there, he'd be so good looking and sing so good it would start a fight. A guy would buy his best girl nice things and maybe dinner. Then he'd get the finest Scotch whiskey to sit on the table and wear his best suit and everything. Well, Johnnie would hit the stage in a fine suit and that cocky, little hat with the feather in it and start singing, *It's Cheaper to Keep Her*, or one of his many other hits, and the place would go wild. The ladies couldn't help themselves, and they'd be fanning their dresses at him and doing other lewd things. You could see the guys getting hotter under their starched collars by the minute. Before long, remarks would fly from table to table until someone would stand up and throw that first punch. Then it did get fun.

Now over in West Memphis, there was The El Toro Club owned by Louis Jack Berger, an old chum of mine, who's Dad had owned The Plantation Inn before progress declared there must be a bigger parking lot for Louis Jack's new restaurant, "Pancho's." Here the hit band, "The Hombres" were featured along with their smash, *Let It All Hang Out*. You could also gamble at some places on Eighth Street in West Memphis, or you could go north of Memphis, out to Tipton County to The Sands or The Turf Club and do damn near anything you wanted to do. The bands there played behind chicken wire until the sun was well up on the Delta. Buford Pusser hung out there, and he "wasn't no sissy."

One Friday night, The Mar-Keys played a gig at The Sands and the next night when we went back for the Saturday gig, the place had been dynamited. The roof was flat down on the ground, and concrete blocks were all the way out to the highway. Luckily, everybody but Terry had taken their stuff home for the night. He had to get a new set of drums. His were flat as a flitter.

When my regular gig at The Rebel Room was over at about one a.m., I wound up most nights downstairs at The Peppermint Lounge playing for free with none other than sax great, Fat Sonny. Johnny Cash would stop by occasionally and sing a few songs. That's how popular the place was.

I loved playing with Fat Sonny. As soon as our gig was done upstairs, whoever was blowin' sax with Paul Richie and me would begin playing, *When The Saints Go Marchin' In*. We would start a parade around the room with everybody struttin' and callin' out, "Follow us!!" We'd march out into the parking lot, go around the building, out to the highway and then along the side of the club until we came to the door leading down to The Peppermint Lounge. There, Fat Sonny and the boys would carry on with *Saints* until everyone was in and swinging. It was loads of fun and no wonder hard to leave.

On the nights when Johnny Cash or Charlie Rich came in, we'd all make sure to get a pill from somewhere, because the raging would continue to four a.m. downstairs. There were other goodies as well. Often, Mr. Williams and Big Mama would be in the crowd, and bootleg would be flowing. It was all right, because there were plenty of politicians around to "fix" anything that might happen. The old, Italian Senator Talarico was one of them. He always sat at the same table every night. If he wasn't there, they left it empty. When he was there, he had a fifth of Old Charter with him and ordered a bowl of ice and a lemon. That was his way, and he never varied it. As the years went by, the old Senator's drinks got a little stronger and his eyes a little waterier. He tended to call more often requesting that Buster allow the band to come to Nashville for private parties at the Hermitage Hotel or his conference room in the State Capitol. Once he sent the State plane to bring us to Nashville. We played at the Governor's Mansion all night and got home around noon the next day. He gave us all one hundred-dollar bills as we were leaving. Since that covered my note and utilities for a month, I was happy. No telling what that plane and pilot cost, but that was long ago. Gas was cheap.

So yes, Memphis rocked in the Sixties!

And one night in 1963, the single most important phone call of my professional life came. I was leaning against the doorframe in our kitchen looking out at my neighbor working in his vegetable garden when the phone rang. On the other end was the jubilant voice of Steve Cropper who'd been out at the club the night before.

"Hey, Wayne," said Steve, almost laughing, he sounded so happy. "How ya' doin' guy?"

"Fine," I said, glad to hear his voice. "How are you?"

"I'm doin' great, man." Steve always was great. "Say, how'd you like to come over and make a record with us this afternoon?"

"I'd love to Steve. Can I leave for the club by eight-thirty?"

"Sure," he said. "If you want to."

And that's how it started.

If I'd been listening a little harder, I might have heard the big engine crank up. I was in for the ride of my life.

College At McLemore

My trumpet tone was sweet the first time I played a note. Bright and airy with a dark streak running down the middle. It's good like that all the way up and down. I play from the bottom of my feet to the end of my nose. And I don't know why, but there is a tiny tremor in it, too. I laugh and say, "There's a tear in every tone."

The saxophone is closest to the human voice, and Andrew Love's sound is as human and warm as he is, solid and wide-set like his shoulders and deep and soulful as his eyes. His sound could coax a bluebird down from the sky.

The very first time we played together we knew something special was going on. We smiled a lot.

Andrew came to Stax after Gilbert Caples got drunk and began to show up late and not remember his parts. He had been working over at Hi with Willie Mitchell, as had drummer, Al Jackson. I knew about Andrew and his tone from hearing him play at the Manhattan Club, so when Al suggested him, I was in agreement.

Add Floyd Newman, with his soft, mildly biting tone and jazz articulation and you have a defining sound of Stax Records...The Horns. Along with Steve Cropper's unmistakable guitar, Duck Dunn's heartbeat bass, Booker T. Jones' magic touch on the Hammond B-3, Al Jackson, the best drummer put on earth, and there it is...Stax.

I was so green I thought all drummers sounded like Al. Yeah! The same for Booker. I'd played with Steve and Duck in the Mar-Keys and always thought they were great. As it turned out, they were my classmates at College and McLemore (the Stax building location), and we shared some wonderful professors! We all learned together. I think Floyd Newman was my favorite. He and Bowlegs, but Bo wasn't at Stax every day like the rest of us.

Everything I needed to make it through the music business, I learned right there. They taught me to use the Magic Wand my mother had been inspired to give me.

We were somehow chosen by fate to be the ONES. The ones of our time to make an impact on popular music, seldom done in history.

I was day walking through my wildest dream.

Duck and I were born on the same day in the same hospital and are both left-handed. Moreover, we both started off playing guitar. Andrew and David Porter were born two days before us. Steve, one month earlier. Coincidence?

I began to consider astrology.

We weren't amazed though. It was just who was there every day. We couldn't have gauged the depth of the talent around us if we'd tried. Let alone the depth of our own.

Songwriter David Porter was there from the beginning. He worked across the street at the grocery store and sold insurance on the side. After that, he came over to the studio and wrote songs. He was so full of life. Teeth and eyes and swirling note paper. I related to him. Go, go, go, hustle, baby, hustle! If that's what it took, I had it, too! David was so real and so positive, and that's what makes soul. We became good friends.

When Isaac Hayes showed up something else happened. Magic. He and David hit it off.

Isaac was poor. Nobody was from more than a middle class family. But Isaac was really poor. He lived with his grandmother on the outskirts of town, and some nights when it was too late to get home, he slept in the back seat of cars. He learned to play piano, because he needed a job and told the bandleader at the Southern Club he could play. So he did...quietly at first. He sang well, too, and crowds liked his deep, bass voice. He was a trip, and like the rest of us, was having fun just being where a chance of something happening was. Nobody, but anybody, knew how much.

From the success of *Gee Whiz, Last Night, Green Onions,* and *You Don't Miss Your Water,* Jim Stewart had to spend some money or give it to Uncle Sam, so he bought the little electronics shop next door and made that East Memphis Music Publishing Company, which housed a couple of writers' rooms and an office. Oh, boy! Romper-rooms! If you were a staffer or an artist, you got a key.

We made records daily. Not much in the evening though, because most of us had night gigs in order to make enough money to live. But after the clubs closed down, the ones who wanted to write would be at it until dawn. Then home for a nap and shower and back at Stax by eleven to begin again.

Duck and I played Lil' Abner's at nine p.m. Many nights his Ford Fairlane was our rocket ride to work and our dressing room, too. More often than not, nights went like this...

Eight p.m. The session would wind down, and we'd listen to the final playback of the day or decide that one more take wouldn't fix it and call it quits, which Steve and Jim loathed to do. But Duck and I would exchange nervous looks. They didn't know what it was like to be late at Buster's.

Eight twenty-five p.m. "Okay, you guys can go."

Duck and I would already be packed up and ready except for latching our cases and putting on our coats. Then...BANG! The big, theater sized, double doors leading out onto McLemore would burst open. Duck and I were headed for the Ford in the parking lot across the street. We took one car so one guy could drive while the other changed clothes in the back seat. Then at the red light at Parkway and Bellevue just after the railroad tracks, the doors would fly open, and the switch was made. The other guy drove like a bat out of hell the last two miles to the club while the new guy in the back seat tore his clothes off, pulled his black suit off the hanger and "dressed."

We prayed for green lights. When we got there, we would skid into the parking lot as close to the stage entrance as possible. After scrambling out of the car and arriving at the stage door, red-faced and sweating, we would pause for a deep breath and look at each other.

"How do I look?"

"Fine, how do I look?"

"Fine. My tie straight?"

"Yeah, mine?"

"Yeah, let's go."

And we'd calmly walk into the club.

Buster loved to intimidate musicians, and when we were late, he saw a fine opportunity. As was his habit, he would sit in the booth nearest the bandstand, facing the door Duck and I would enter, thumping the heel of his well-shined shoe on its linoleum underpinning and clicking his false teeth together under his beak of a nose. When we came through the door, he would exclaim in a loud voice, "Glad we could get together!"

Meanwhile, Andrew was wherever Bowlegs was, and Al Jackson played various club gigs. Steve was usually writing songs with the artist of the day at the motel where they were staying. Sometimes I was with them writing horn parts. And Isaac and David were busy taking inspiration wherever they could get it.

Once David was in the restroom, and Isaac hollered, "Come on David! Hurry up!" And David answered, "Hold On I'm Comin'!".....The truth.

Dave Prater and Sam Moore at Stax

The artist roster was building, and more and more of our time was required. Nobody cared how many hours we were there, because we weren't on salary yet. But if we got more songs cut, we got more sixty-five dollar session fees. We were getting increasingly proficient at the process of making songs go together, too, so sometimes we actually got a session fee in one day. Often though, we left saying, "we owe you one, okay," and we'd come back the next morning and begin again where we left off. It was the way it was, and we didn't mind. Hell, we were making more money than we'd ever made in our lives and having fun at it. And when you work like that, nobody really knows where you are all the time, so the opportunities for monkey business were always there. And we were monkeys.

Andrew and I would look at each other and say, "WHAT ARE WE GONNA DO WHEN THIS IS ALL OVER, OPEN A BAIT SHOP?" We'd laugh like hell, but we were serious. We always said if it didn't change for the better in another year, we'd stop and get jobs. The trouble was something always happened to pull us in for one more year. Which was easy, after all, what in hell were we gonna do? I didn't even have a high school degree, and Andrew had one year of college. Who were we kidding? And every year the stew thickened. We both had growing families. A son, Duane Lamar Jackson, had come to Linda and I. The grandparents took the blond, green-eyed baby over much the way they did Carla. He was a happy baby, and because he liked to scoot backwards, I dubbed him "Scooter."

My royalties were beginning to increase, and I wrote songs for the Mar-Keys' albums and some for other Stax artists I backed like Sam and Dave, Eddie Floyd, Albert King, Carla Thomas, Johnnie Taylor, Booker T. & the MGs and The Willie Mitchell band.

I got my first new car in 1965, a new '64 Mercury Comet Caliente. It was a gold, two-door, straight stick with leather seats and a sporty, little, radio antenna on the rear fender. I remember the day I got it and stopped in at Pat's Lounge to show Dad. He was so proud, kinda like I had graduated or something. I was somebody, even to the guys Dad always drank beer with.

Each year, there'd be several occasions where I could walk through our front door on McCauley and say something like, "Good news, honey, they're releasing that Eddie Floyd song I wrote with Cropper as a single in Europe" or "We're doin' another Mar-Keys album next week."

Our growing savings account reflected that all was going well. It acted as a shield between me and Linda when she said, "And just where in the hell have YOU been 'til six o'clock this morning?"

My comings and goings around my house were unusual for the neighborhood, to say the least, and although I didn't know it, the West Memphis policeman who lived three houses down from us was watching with mighty suspicion. I was out cutting the grass when everybody else was off at work, and as time went by, the cars in my driveway got longer and wider. And when I got the brand new, red 1967 Riviera with the white leather interior, it was too much.

I'd just had the car a week or so when he stopped me.

I was coming back from Mom's house where I'd been for a visit and was within a block of home when he pulled in behind me and turned on his spinning, blue lights and bumped his siren. I couldn't imagine anything I'd done, and when I saw who it was, I figured he wanted to talk to me about the kids or something.

I pulled over to the curb and rolled down the window, as he sauntered up to the glistening car. He leaned down and looked in at the white leather as he adjusted the heavy, black belt with the thirty-eight special and mace hanging off it.

"Well," he said, "whose car is this?"

I was dumbfounded. My eyes narrowed, and I felt a little coldness in my gut.

"Mine," I said. He was scowling.

"You got the papers?"

"Sure," I replied and reached to open the glove box where the registration was kept. What the hell is this all about, I thought. Then I remembered telling my daughter Carla not to hang around his daughter too much, since she was five years older, and I thought she had a mean look about her. Besides, there were lots of girls Carla's age in the neighborhood. Our street was full of kids.

"Here you are." I said. "Anything wrong?"

"Just wondering about the car. Where'd you get it?"

"Down the street at Chalmers' Buick."

"Uh, huh."

I didn't say anything else. I think the color drained from my face a little as I realized he lived close by but knew nothing of me or my life. And after the thing with his daughter, he could give me grief, except I'd done nothing wrong and felt as safe as you can with a West Memphis, Arkansas, cop breathing in your face.

He handed back the papers and said, "All right, I was just curious."

I said I'd see him later and went on home, just two blocks from where we'd been sitting, but by the time I got there I felt the hot sting of tears in my eyes. Just what kind of garbage was this, I thought. I was getting madder and madder and feeling helpless. This would never happen in a bigger town, I thought. I was weak with emotion, but as I saw him pull in his driveway just down the street, I knew that most nights if he had stopped me and been mad, he could have found pills. And I'd probably have been drinking. Damn, I thought.

The storm door on the red brick, story and a half house flew open and a trio of little boys came bowling out into the front yard and ran by the nose of the Buick. My son, Scooter, and his pals, Jo-Jo and Bullet, the neighborhood gang, were looking for a back yard to explore. A getaway from the Mamas. The door hissed shut, silencing the country music playing softly on the kitchen radio.

Linda was lying on the bed watching TV when I walked in. She just barely glanced my way as I opened the louvered, closet doors and began looking through the clothes, pulling out the sleeves of various suits.

"Goin' to the studio?"

"Yeah. Otis is back in town."

"What time?"

"Oh, after dinner."

"Mama and Daddy are comin' over after awhile. They're takin' one of those things off Daddy's nose this afternoon, and Mama's gonna rest him here before they go back."

"Great," I said. Mr. and Mrs. Christopher, the salt of the earth, usually brought empty, one-gallon milk jugs to fill up with water when they came. Their water was okay for some things but had too much iron in it for drinking or washing clothes. I loved them as much as my own folks. We'd lived on the farm with them at various stages of our growing up, and they thought our kids were theirs. Carla called Mr. Christopher "Daddy" and me "Daddy Wayne." Mrs. Christopher would just laugh.

Out the bedroom window across the street, I saw our neighbor Shelly in a halter-top and shorts with big, green gloves on, bent over pulling weeds from the new grass. What a woman, I thought. I couldn't control my wandering eyes in my own bedroom.

Linda didn't let on that she'd noticed.

I threw the clothes I'd selected across the foot of the bed, and as Linda got up to go in the kitchen to begin preparing dinner, I undressed and went into the bathroom for a shower. I heard Carla come in from school and shout "Hey!" as she climbed the stairs to her bedroom.

The Christophers arrived with "Daddy" gingerly touching a bandage that ran across his nose. Mama sat him down on the green, nawgahide, living room couch while she went in to help with dinner. I sat down with him and asked about his skin cancer and things on the farm. "It's the sun," he said, fingering the bandage. He was outside from before dawn until after dark. He was a man of few words, like actor Gary Cooper. In fact, he looked like him.

"How's your work agoin'?"

I tried to tell him, but I don't think he really understood what it was I did. He knew I "made music," but couldn't imagine "my work." He was just glad I had a job, no matter how mysterious. Out on the farm, he'd tune up his old guitar once in awhile and make an "axe handle G," as he put it, and strum with his callused thumb, while humming and singing little bits of some half-remembered, hillbilly song.

"Fine, Daddy, we're busy this week," was about all I ever replied.

We ate early. Everybody was used to me working at night, so no one minded when I excused myself and finished dressing on the way out the front-door, kissing kids and saying goodbye as I headed for the shiny, red Buick, smiling to myself with anticipation. I was eager to show off at College and McLemore.

I drove across the Memphis/Arkansas bridge thinking that I'd better go home the back way that night to avoid another unwanted confrontation. In fact, every night from now on.

When I reached McLemore, I drove slowly by the studio and soaked up the cat calls from the pedestrian, soul brothers standing out on the street waiting for Otis to show up. The street locals always knew when he or one of the other stars was about to arrive and would gang up on the sidewalk in front of Stax and hang around. Sometimes the Mad Lads would get a shoeshine job out of it. The excitement was always there, and I added to it with my new car.

"Wooooooo, BIG BUCKS! WE KNOW WHO'S GETTING AAAALLL THE MONEY!" They laughed and jeered, pointing at me as I drove by. It was delicious like a big apple pie, and I was a slice.

I drove into the grocery store parking lot across the street, circled around and came back to park, angled into the curb. I let the big, wildcat engine run a few seconds for effect before shutting it off and getting out with a smile. I went to the trunk and got my trumpet amid calls of "Get DOWN!" and "Now ain't that SOMETHIN' else!"

We'd been making hit records around there for enough years that all the musicians were folk heroes, and I played it to the hilt. I knew everybody.

I was laughing and slapping hands with the Mad Lads lead singer, Julius Green, when down McLemore Street came Steve Cropper and Otis in Steve's green, '65 Riviera and pulled in next to my newer one. They were all smiles as they got out.

"Man, DAMN, whatcha' got here?" asked Otis, as he looked my car up and down, grinning that huge grin of his and grabbing me around the shoulders. "Man! How you doin'? How 'bout a ride in that sheen!?" He was doing that backward scoot, all bent over, dragging me with him.

I laughed and twisted away, "Don't we have to get workin'?" I asked. "Yeah," said Cropper, catching the mood of the moment, "but why don't y'all go get a bucket of fried chicken first? I'll hook up the studio while your gone." It was all the excuse we needed. Otis went around and got in the passenger side and off we went. "You wanna drive?" I asked.

"Naw," he said, "man, this here's a helluva machine. When'd ja get it?" He was squeezing the leather and rubbing the dashboard, peering into the back seat. All the while gently rocking back and forth and pumping his right heel up and down. Pretty, new stuff excited Otis. Under his immaculate mustache showed every tooth in his head, which lit up the whole scene. I could tell he was fired up, more than usual, and it was going to be a thrilling night in the studio.

There was a Kentucky Fried Chicken just around the corner on Bellevue that was sandwiched in between two other buildings. There was very little parking space in front, but I managed to squeeze the gleaming car in between two others. I started to get out and said to Otis, "Why don't you just sit tight while I get the chicken?" I was feeling a little protective of my friend.

"Naw," he grinned, "you know I gotta go!"

The truth was there were several dark-skinned gals in cute, little uniforms and caps behind the glass, and Otis could not resist any chance to flirt! So he got out, too, and up to the window, we strolled.

A girl in a starched, white, short dress came over. "Can I help you?" she purred, putting the order pad on the counter top. Her eyes drifted upward to the hulking presence beside me and after a second or two froze. Her head was slightly down, and those eyes bugged outward and upward.

Slowly, the word spread throughout the building all the way into the kitchen about the customer up front, and faces with frozen smiles began to appear from every window and door. The cook came out holding a basket of sizzling french fries and just stood there...sizzling.

Otis said with a chuckle, "Could we get a bucket of that good, crispy chicken?" and he grinned even bigger.

Nothing happened.

I could smell burning nylon and oozing testosterone. This could be a mess.

"Yes, MAM!" I said.

Otis was leaning on his elbows on the counter sill and knew exactly what he was causing! He loved it.

Suddenly, as if on cue, the whole place came to life.

People walked into each other and stammered, and the french fry girl dropped her potato cage.

Then there appeared a large bucket of chicken, and the girl asked without taking her huge eyes off Otis, "What would you like to drink?"

"Six large, cold drinks," he replied. "Cokes."

She tore herself away and started getting big cokes and putting them in a sack. Then another large bucket of crispy, fried chicken showed up in the window.

When she brought the Cokes, I asked, "How much?"

The girl managed, "Eight dollars."

There were four girls now standing behind girl number one, all grinning like they were peeing in their pants.

"That's it?" I asked. It seemed to be a lot of food for eight bucks.

"That's it," she purred, staring intently at Otis. All of them could have been singing, "Here I am baby."

I handed Otis the drink sacks and told him to put them in the car, which he did, and I followed with the two buckets.

As I got in and started the car, he was laughing loud. He slapped his knee and said, "Boy that's FUN!" He kept on laughing. I was laughing, too. With Otis, you just couldn't help but have a good time. More fun than I could remember having!

We got back to Stax with two buckets of fried chicken and two big sacks of large, cold drinks. We held the stuff close in front of us as we went through the cheering gang on the sidewalk outside.

Steve was standing in his usual spot, dead center of the room, Telecaster strung around his neck, legs held tightly together and a grin on his face. "Wow, look at this! I hope you left some for the home folks!" Everybody laughed at the amount of chicken we had, but Otis didn't like small anything. Everything about him was bigger than life, fried chicken included.

Duck put down his bass, Al got off the drums and Booker and Isaac rose from the keyboards. Andrew, Floyd and Joe put down their horns. Everyone had been doodling and warming up, catching the pitch off Duck's bass. Now, we all began to attack the chicken and talk at once. "Where's the hot sauce?" asked Al. He ate hot sauce on everything.

The talk was of road battles and mis-adventures, combined with the homeboys renditions of Arabian nights on the local club scene, all blending together into a sort of "big-boys-toys" contest.

When Jim pushed the button that let him hear the noise on the floor, instead of talk about his next big hit, he got an earful of loud contest. He had grown a thick, red mustache and to his credit had not pulled it out yet, but he tugged at it a lot. The more we laughed, the redder his face got, and the more he tugged. The follicles must have been sore all the time.

I remember once me and Andrew, Floyd and Bowlegs were standing behind the partition, and something happened within this particular song that made Jim stop the tape. I made the comment, "Do we need to play that lick again?" That's what I remember. And Jim Stewart hit that talk-back switch and said, "Yes, you do." I spread my arms and said, "Well, I just thought I'd ask."

It really tickled everybody on the floor. They laughed their heads off. They thought that was hysterical. Of course, Jim turned red in the control room, and I'm sure he hated me even worse after that. As a fiddle player, he didn't like horns anyway. And he certainly didn't like people having a good time playing a horn.

Tonight, he blushed and pushed the talk-back switch and said, "Come on guys, will you? We've got lots to do."

We finished our dinner, wiped the grease off our hands and got ready for Otis to show us what he wanted to do. Since this was an old movie theater with the seats removed and carpet laid down, the floor slanted downward from the entry door to the end where the control room was situated. That meant we always played going downhill or uphill depending on which way you faced. We were used to it, and it didn't hurt anything. Maybe it contributed to the room sound. In fact, I think it did.

We took our positions, and Otis picked up his little rhythm guitar, put one foot up in a chair and started strumming. It was tuned to "open E," so he didn't have to actually finger chords, just hold down all the strings along a bar fret. It would automatically be a chord and by moving up or down on the fret bar, he could change the chord up or down. It worked.

"This here's a little song I been workin' on, y'all," he spoke/croaked with a rural Georgia, country slang. Then he shocked us all.

"It's called *The Tennessee Waltz*!"

I played that song every night at the Rebel Room, but never like this! After we got into it, Otis staggered around the room with his fists held up to the heavens, singing our state anthem to the ceiling, and his soul radiated through us like ringing a bell. It's not natural to play the trumpet and smile at the same time, but I swear I did.

In the control room, Al Bell and Jim were bowled over. "It can't get any funkier than THAT!" laughed Al.

Otis was fun!

No matter who was cutting, Sam and Dave, Wilson Pickett or Albert King, the question on our lips was, "When's Otis coming?"

Not that the others weren't fun! When Albert King was in doing *Born Under A Bad Sign*, he played so good Duck shrugged off his bass and threw it to the floor, screaming, "GaaaaawdDAAAMN!" Then Al Jackson quit, and everyone else did, too, just laughing 'til we came back to our senses and could continue. Big Albert King acted like he didn't know what had happened. Yeah!

I don't know if Jim Stewart enjoyed that as much as everybody else did, but he tried.

We carried the joy of those studio days through our lives. In the clubs at night or on the golf course, we were "the guys." We made the records everybody loved, it was common knowledge, and when any of us played somewhere, no matter where, people expected us to shine. And we did!

I'd go from a session to my gig and give a million-dollar performance every time. The groove from the day just wouldn't turn me loose, like Otis said. Many nights, Duck and Joe Arnold would be there, too, with the house band, and we'd rock those hillbillies so hard they didn't know what hit them. The dance floor would be jammed with wildly, gyrating locals, benefiting from the groove set up by Stax artists during the day, and they didn't want to leave 'til after four a.m.

The turning point for the club thing came in early 1967 when I found out we were going to Europe with the Stax/Volt Revue, put together by Atlantic Records.

"Give me two cheeseburgers and make my buns greasy" was the catch phrase at Slim Jenkins Joint two doors down to the left of Stax Records. It was a dark and seedy place that suited the neighborhood perfectly and was the rendezvous point for the musicians headed to work in the studio.

On this particular day, the conversation at our table was steeped with excitement.

"We're going to Europe?" asked Andrew.

"Yep," answered Steve. "Jim told me Atlantic Records is putting together a big tour for us over there. They're going to call it The Stax/Volt Revue. Otis is already the number one male vocalist in England, you know."

"Who all's going?" I asked in an awed voice.

"I think just about everybody," said Steve. "All of us, and I know for sure Otis, Sam and Dave, Carla, Eddie Floyd. It'll be a hell of a show."

"How long will we be gone?"

"About a month."

"I'll bet Newman won't be able to get out of school that long," said Andrew. "It's his last year at Memphis State."

"Well, you'll figure it out," said Steve. "Y'all are the horns, but I think you need a third."

"Why don't we just take Joe," Duck suggested. "He's been doing the sessions anyway."

"Yeah," said Andrew. "We could do that. Two tenors and a trumpet would work fine. Why don't you ask him when you get to work tonight,Wayne."

"I will, I will." But I was already wondering how we could get away from Hernando's Hideaway for that long and still have a job when we got back. Joe and I had been working there together six nights a week for over a year and had developed a pretty respectable following. The owner, Gordon Reid, would not take kindly to the thought of us being gone a whole month.

Lunch was now over, and the four of us walked out in the sunny, but windy, cold, January afternoon and stood there for a moment watching the traffic go by. The few remaining autumn leaves clung desperately to the branches of the trees across the street.

"Whoever's going has to be on board by next week. We're going down to Lansky Brothers to get fitted for some new suits. We need to get passport pictures taken too, so get to it."

New suits and passport pictures, I thought. Damn, we're really going.

"See you later," Duck yelled as he and Steve went through the swinging doors of the studio leaving Andrew and I standing at the curb where our cars were parked.

"Man, do you believe that," laughed Love. "Suits and everything."

"As a matter of fact I don't! Europe!"

Later when I asked Gordon, the club owner, if I could have the month off to go to Europe with the Stax Volt Revue and have my job when I got back, he said, "No." A big mistake for him, but a lesson for me.

In my life, everything happens for a reason and for the best.

Back at Stax, the atmosphere was charging up. The coming tour had everybody excited and talking constantly about nothing else. Andrew and I were told we'd be making two thousand dollars for the month and all expenses. That was a lot of money. We were also told that since Floyd Newman couldn't make it, Joe Arnold was definitely going. That meant we'd be light on the bottom end, but since it would be live and loud, we thought nobody would notice.

We were all to go down to Lansky Brothers on Beale Street and get fitted for some hip suits.

It was a beautiful afternoon when we got there, and they were ready. Bernard Lansky grabbed us and yanked us through the door. He was grinning as he looked us up and down and hustled us past the racks of ready made silk and mohair suits, toward the curtained-off fitting room in the back with the famous "fitting platform" where "E" himself had stood so many times.

"Man, I'm gonna have you guys lookin' like the toast of the town! Nothin' but the finest! Jim Stewart said to outfit y'all with not one but TWO suits! Here Jackson, get up here where I fit Elvis in all HIS clothes."

He was proud of that and justly so. It's where Elvis bought his wild, honky-tonk stuff, and we all knew it.

Andrew and I had our clothes custom made down the street at Paul's Custom Suits, once a month until our closets were bulging. And with each suit, Paul gave us a tailored shirt with our initials on the cuff, so we had plenty of our own brand of show stuff. But Lansky's was a whole different animal.

"What kind of material y'all thinkin' about? I tell ya, though, this mohair is sharp! Double sharp! I mean those girls will be tryin' to tear it off y'all the minute y'all walk out on stage, guaranteed! Y'all hear me? Guaranteed!"

He had a raw suit going on my shoulders, and it was electric blue. There was so much energy in it I felt like jumping up and down. We were all grinning as he tugged and pinned and soaped. "This is YOU, this is YOU!! It's YOU, man," he said, "am I kiddin'? Am I lyin' to ya? Is this the greatest thing you ever had on in your life? You married Jackson? It don't make a shit, all the girls gonna LOVE you...I'm serious! Look at this COLOR! Am I lying?"

So we looked into the triple mirrors. Holy God! Zoot suit blue! Bernard was ecstatic! "I got this number in cat-eyed green, too! All wool to the bone! Hey! You guys gonna take over Europe, man, in MY clothes! Mohair from Lansky's! I don't think even Elvis got this suit! I mean it! Would I lie to ya?"

Then it was Andrew and Joe's turn, and we laughed as Bernard did what made his life a wondrous thing.

"I'm not kiddin'! You guys think I'm KIDDIN' but I am not KIDDIN'! You guys are gonna make 'em crazy for you in these suits, you watch what I tell ya! By the way, y'all need shoes?"

Finally, the fitting session was over, and the exhausted Mar-Key horns were about to leave the building.

"Hey! Wait a minute! What you guys gonna wear WITH these gorgeous new suits you got? T-shirts? NO! Not while I got breath! Come over here and let me show you something brand new! It's the craze!"

We left with striped turtlenecks. They matched both suits, and we loved them. As for shoes, we were into Beatle boots, and that's what we wore.

The weeks passed full of excited anticipation. None of us musicians had been to Europe, and who knew if we'd ever go again. So we talked and planned, dreamed and talked, and talked some more. What would the food be like? Would the water in France really make us sick? The hotels? Would they be first class? The transportation? Who WAS King Tours anyway? And mostly, the "Birds." What would THEY be like, and more importantly, would they dig US?

I bought a Super 8 home movie camera and a ton of color film in fifty-foot rolls, and an Instamatic to go with it. I loved photography, and this was as good an excuse as I'd likely get to splurge. I should have felt guilty, running around like a chicken with its head cut off all excited and buying stuff for the adventure of a lifetime and just about ignoring my family. If Linda wanted to go or was jealous, she never said anything. Maybe there'd be other times, I said. I wasn't being mean or anything. They just weren't taking wives.

It turned out to be a good thing. We did twenty-nine cities in thirty-one days!

There were immense preparations going on in New York and Europe that we were totally unaware of. At home we just continued on our same hectic path of recording and rampaging through Memphis. They were trying to get product ready for the European market to coincide with the tour though, and photograph sessions were sprinkled in with the rest of the hubbub for good measure. It was all a blur of songs and excitement.

The one thing we didn't do was rehearse.

MEM

Atlantic Crossing

We were a family on our first European vacation together, and we were excited. None of us in the band had ever been before, and all we could think about was that soon we would be landing in London! England!

Duck and I had our Super 8 cameras loaded with film and the Instamatics, too. We were ready for Freddie. Click, whir, click, whir! We took pictures of everything we'd probably never see again...clouds, Russian airliners, each other, each other's jewelry and stewardesses.

And that was just on the way over!

Were we thinking we'd never see that again? Kids on vacation.

We were a little hung over, but too excited to notice much as we struggled through customs with our gear. Out on the sidewalk, there was silent jubilation as we waited on transport to the hotel. Suddenly, a truck pulled up with someone who knew our names and behind it a line of limos, black and shining in the cold, morning sun. They were Bentleys owned by the Beatles themselves! Each with a driver in dark, blue livery sent to pick us up out of respect. WOW!

Otis was pointing and laughing, and soon we all were. We were hunched over with our hands down in our pockets from the cold, but we were laughing! There was scrambling for seats, and I wound up in the middle of a back seat with my trumpet in my lap. And Andrew and Joe squeezed in on either side of me. We were grinning like monkeys of some kind, but it didn't matter. We'd made it.

At the Mayfair Hotel, we walked into the lobby with lots of good-natured shoving and laughing and were standing around in a knot when someone yelled in a clipped accent, "God, that's the QUEEN!"

The entire pack of us jammed back out through the smallish doors onto the sidewalk, nearly crushing one another, cameras held high over our heads, snapping away at any black car that happened by and jumping up and down to get a glimpse. That is, until we heard the distinct sound of snickering coming from the bell stand. We'd been had and good in the "welcome to merry old England, Yanks" style! We found out later it was the bell stands fondest sport!

Finally, we got checked in and had just a few minutes to freshen up a bit

Eddie Floyd, Sam Moore, Steve Cropper, Wayne & Otis, Arthur Conley at the London airport

before being rushed over to Polydor Studios for a grueling, eight hour rehearsal. We'd not played many of the songs since recording them, in some cases years before. So we played and furiously made notes, one artist after another.

Then somehow we lost the notes! Joe, Andy and I talked it over and decided there was nothing to do but go ahead like nothing was wrong instead of telling and then looking like the fools we felt like.

The next day we rehearsed at Rymuse Studio, and it was a marathon again. This time we kept the notes but had a severe sense of foreboding like we'd never remember all this stuff no matter WHAT we did. And we were right. There was something like thirty-two songs! That's too much to ask of anybody, but the three of us just shrugged and acted like we were fine with it. We would rely on insane whisperings and hand signals to get through the first shows until we got a feel for how it all lay and how much we could remember.

As it turned out, we surprised ourselves by remembering a lot. Whether out of fear of reprisals from above or the "just do it" thing, I don't 'til this day know, but whatever lesson we learned, it has served us well.

The next day was Wednesday, and that night there was a big press reception at the famous nightclub, the Speakeasy, hangout for loads of English rock stars like the Stones. Jet lag was firmly in place, and the liquor flowed. We had never experienced that combination and didn't relate the two, unfortunately. We answered tons of questions when we were asked, though, and tried to look important as the sometimes center of attention before an English-sounding press. They were SO interested in us all! We stayed there as long as somebody was asking questions. Too long!

Thursday, we were in a cloud and tried to sleep late, but excitement got us. We arose early and went sightseeing. We trudged around London as long as our heavy feet would allow and then returned to the hotel. Ganged up in Andrew's room before dinner, we reviewed the notes we had and tried to remember what we could about the music. We tried, but it was not much use. Our brains were too tired and "what the hell" had descended upon us.

Opening night arrived, and the excitement in the air was touchable. We were to be at the Astoria Theater in Finsbury Park. I think about two thousand souls and us. It was sold out! I didn't do much thinking. My mind was frozen with thoughts of the unthinkable...like brain freeze or fainting when the music started.

When we arrived, the crowd was snaking all down beside the theater, and it was cold outside. These people wanted to see us bad. They had grins on their faces, and pound notes clutched in their fists, excitedly talking among themselves. When our cars pulled up at the stage door around in the alley, hundreds of folks were there shouting, "Otis, Otis," and waving pieces of paper for autographs, which they did not get.

We felt like the Beatles at Shea Stadium in New York! The turmoil, the screaming, the reaching out to touch.

And us looking out the window at wild-eyed expectants looking back and leaning into the blue uniformed cops holding them back with linked arms. It was incredible. The high from it indescribable. I was floating and holding onto things as we got out and started up the steps to backstage where more pandemonium awaited.

As soon as we were inside, the band, Booker T. & the MGs and the Mar-Keys, went on to warm up, find mike positions and get a little feel for that particular stage. Then it was rehearsal or "sound check" time. We all got to run through our songs for the sound system and lighting people. Booker and the guys did *Green Onions* and *Bootleg*. They were great! We had an easy time with our songs, too, *Last Night* and the song Andrew and I wrote with Floyd Newman, *Grab This Thing*.

Then the trouble started.

One by one our troop of wonderful artists began coming on stage and doing their set, usually their big (and only) hit, which we generally knew, and one or two off their albums that Stax was trying to promote over there. That's when the wild whispering and gesturing began. Thank God, nobody noticed, maybe because they were scrambling themselves, but we didn't notice them either! Sweat was pouring freely by then on that cool stage.

When Sam and Dave came out they were like real pros. They sang and pranced around a bit, but not too much, saving themselves for the double show that evening. This calmed us a little, and we made it through just fine, being able to hear the insane hissings and squawks of each other during our on-stage arranging. Sam and Dave smiled sweetly at us as they departed, trying to step over their own puddles of sweat.

We breathed a sigh of relief. We knew they would turn it all the way up come show time.

Finally, Otis came on, and I've never seen a person like that then or since! He looked like a double pile driver with thirty-two, huge glistening teeth, dressed in slacks and a sweater, stomping up and down from heaven to hell and back, and we suffered with him. I still don't know how many songs he did, but we only knew about half.

When his sound check was finished, Otis came over and put his elbows on top of my shoulders. "Well," he purred, "you guys all right over here?" He laughed his graveled laugh, and the heat off his body nearly melted my leather coat.

"Sure," we said. We were a little sheepish, but we knew everything was cool. And we knew, HE knew! My knees were sagging, and I was glad when he got off me. Damn, he was a big guy.

Andrew, Joe and I then went to the dressing room where our bags and horns cases were and changed into our Lansky Brothers suits for the show. We didn't talk much, because we were nervous. And there was absolutely nothing we could do about it. Faith was placed where faith had to be, and so it was cast.

The show was broken down into two halves, and it would provide us with a short breather to recover and talk a bit about the upcoming horn lines. After all, they were recording this first show, and it sharpened our edge quite a bit.

To say we were fired up would be an understatement of the first order!

When talking time was finished, Booker T. and the MGs got into position, and the house lights dimmed. The crowd was humming, and single voices called out, "Otis, Otis!" or just screamed! The hair was standing up on the back of my neck.

In England, they call the Master of Ceremonies, the Compare, God knows why, but ours was taking the stage. And the crowd noise came up higher in anticipation. His job was to get them going just as hard as he could and announce the various acts as they lined up.

"ALL RIGHT!" he cried, "ARE YOU READY LONDON?"

"YES," the crowd roared.

"COME ON NOW, LET'S GIVE 'EM A BIG LONDON WELCOME! S!"

They responded, "S!"

"T," he cried.

"T!!"

"GIMME AN A!"

And they screamed, "A!"

"AND AN X!"

They shouted, "X!"

"STAX, STAX, STAX!!" he wailed, and they rose to the occasion, "STAX!!! STA X!!! STAX!!!"

"AND HERE TO OPEN THE SOUL SHOW OF THE CENTURY IS BOOKER T. AND THE MGs!!!"

The curtain started up. The house lights dimmed. The spotlight stabbed down through the darkness upon Booker T. and the MGs, and as the white light hit their electric green suits and smiling faces, they dove in!

Red Beans and Rice was their first number, and you'd have thought the audience was brought up on the stuff...they went wild!

They never stopped cheering as the MGs went on to *Booker-Loo* for their second number and then to their classic, first hit, *Green Onions*. When they finished that song, the whole place broke out in wild cheering.

Now, as I looked out on the big, empty stage, I knew it was time. I had never been so aware of recording going on. Tom Dowd had come over with us and scrounged up two three-track machines from somewhere. He was in the basement of the theater with them slaved together, getting every live thing that happened that night. And I knew it was one of those moments in a person's life that makes a difference. Oh God, I prayed silently. This ain't Lil' Abner's Rebel Room!

Joe Arnold, Wayne, Andrew Love

All that was just a rehearsal for this! This is the BIG TIME! And here we go!

Our Compare was saying, "AND NOW FOR THE ICING ON THE SOUL CAKE, THE SOUND THAT MAKES THE WHOLE PICTURE COME TO LIFE, HERE'S WAYNE JACKSON, ANDREW LOVE AND JOE ARNOLD, THE FABULOUS MAR-KEYS!!"

We were all standing up so straight and grinning. We walked out fast onto the stage in our shiny, new, blue suits as the volume of the crowd went up about twenty percent. We didn't say anything, and Al Jackson counted off the first recording of my life from 1961, *Last Night.*

The crowd loved it, and it went very smoothly. When it got to the part where Floyd Newman said, "Ooooh, Last Night," on the original, I leaned down, and being fully aware that my voice would be the one on this recording said, "OOOOH, LAST NIGHT!" I was filled with elation and pride. And I wished my family could have been there.

The cheering was thunderous, and we played our other chart record, *Grab This Thing,* the one Gene Parker played the original sax solo on. Joe Arnold filled in for him and blew a great one!

As we played the final chord and took our musical bows, before fading into our background positions, the Compare came out amid the crazy thunder and began his pitch for the next act, Arthur Conley. The bright spots had left us for the Compare, and one light was toying with the side of the stage where

Arthur would eventually come out. He was Otis' protégé, and the crowd knew it!

Out of the corner of my eye, I could see Arthur standing all alone in the wings over by the curtain, painfully skinny, holding on with one hand and grinning that same, "Oh damn" grin we all had on.

"SAY IT WITH ME NOW, DO YOU LOVE SOUL MUSIC?!"

And they screamed back, "YES, WE LOVE SOUL MUSIC!"

"WE'RE HERE TO GIVE YOU A SOUL FULL TONIGHT! LET ME HEAR HOW YOU FEEL NOW, DO YOU LOVE SOUL MUSIC?!!"
The crowd nearly blew his clothes off with a two thousand strong roar, "YES! WE LOVE SOUL MUSIC!!"

"WELL GET READY THEN, ...CAUSE HERE'S THE SWEET SOUL MUSIC MAN HIMSELF TO GET THIS SOUL TRAIN OUTTA' THE STATION, THE MAN HIMSELF, ARTHUR CONLEY!!"

Arthur raised his arms high and walked briskly onto center stage. We started his music, and he started dancing. The crowd went wild again. He really leaned into his performance and milked the crowd for all it was worth. He sounded rather like Sam Cooke, and he used that, too.

Carla stood in the wings now, and I thought she looked cool and sweet as she waited.

Arthur finished to thunderous applause.

Carla would have to be good, I thought.

She was announced, and with a huge smile on her face, she calmly walked out on stage, swaying her hips in the age-old tradition of beautiful women. The crowd was in love at first sight, and Carla loved them back! She started out with *Something Good,* her new European release, and then went into *Let Me Be Good To You.*

Suddenly, I saw the look on the audiences' faces, and I realized they were incredulous. There we were, all together on the stage at one time! Right before their very eyes. They stood for her this time and clapped like they were seeing a great star.

But she was not through with them yet. Finally, she did her blockbuster hit, *B-A-B-Y,* and they melted for her.

They stood and stomped and hooted, and I thought, okay Eddie, come on!

Now, Eddie Floyd is no lightweight, and on this first show of our

European tour, he took no quarter. He came out with both barrels blazing and sang *Raise Your Hand.* He is a master crowd manipulator and really got them on his side quickly. They were all singing and waving their arms by the time he got through with them. Then he did the tried and true, *If I Had A Hammer*, and the crowd quieted down some. It seemed as if he might loose them that time, but when we started the classic intro to *Knock On Wood*, they came unglued! They poured out into the aisles, dancing and singing the words, jumping up and down! The tide was building into a tidal wave it looked like.

He rocked on and on, strutting from one side of the stage to the other. My face felt like it was going to fall off when he finally sang the last chorus and departed for the last time.

The curtain had come down, and the Compare was telling the crowd, "YOU AIN'T SEEN NOTHIN' YET!!"

They weren't about to go anywhere, though, except out to the lobby to get a beer themselves!

But we didn't care. We staggered to the side of the stage where the drinks were and rubbed our faces and laughed and hugged each other. God this was great! It looked like we were "in!" Could you believe it? The Yanks were giving it back to 'em for the British takeover by the Beatles! US!

Eddie Floyd, ever thoughtful, came over and hugged us, thanking us and getting more sweat on our already soaked suits. Everyone was celebrating, but now it was time for the second half.

Cropper walked by on his way back to the stage, stuck his guitar pick between his teeth and shook my hand first, then Andrew's and Joe's. "By God, that was great," he said, "let's go git 'em again!"

Booker T. and the MGs swung into *Groovin*, and the frenzy started back up. This time it was a constant, loud buzz that went up and down in volume.

I spied Sam and Dave over by the curtain ready to go on. They weren't so calm now. They looked like "Man 'O War" and "Seabiscuit" in the starting gate at Churchill Downs race track, prancing around with nostrils flared and skin jerking from eagerness. Their eyes flashed as they sensed the crowd waiting. They didn't have to wait long.

The guy out front had a hard time being heard as he tried to hawk the duo on stage. But hell, they didn't need hawking! They needed unleashing!

Finally, he just threw up his hands and cried, "SO HERE THEY ARE, SAM AND DAVE!!"

We started into *You Don't Know Like I Know,* and Sam and Dave flew onto center stage like two balls of St. Elmo's Fire, dancing the New York soul dance while holding their pant legs up in front so the crowd could see the foot action!

Bedlam broke out! The audience was a sea of uncontrolled passion, wiggling and screaming like maniacs, dancing where they stood, eyes popping out of their heads and drool hanging from slack mouths. They were drugged.

It never stopped the whole six songs except during *When Something's Wrong With My Baby.* You could hear a pin drop. People were sobbing, including myself. It's still the most moving performance of that song I ever heard, even later in the tour when we all had a better handle on the music. I still think that was the best song ever written.

Sam and Dave were consummate performers and crowd pleasers. They danced, they begged, they ran out in the audience, and the police had to carry them back on stage. And their feet were still dancing. During their last song, *Hold On, I'm Comin',* Dave fainted and had to be carried off. When the crowd begged for more, he miraculously revived and came back, hiking his pants up so he could dance some more. Sweat ran off them in rivers, and we all worked harder than we'd ever worked in our whole lives. How could the heat go up?

Finally, Sam and Dave drug themselves off, their coats on the floor dragging behind them, heads hanging in utter exhaustion for the last time, and the audience, instead of being blown out, would not sit down. They knew what was coming.

I had just witnessed the damnedest show I had ever even heard about, and the stage was still smoking. And my friend was coming on next. I tried not to worry, but damn!

Otis stood on the side of the stage waiting for his moment to arrive. He appeared fairly calm, gazing down at the floor and hitching up his shoulders occasionally. But I knew he was six sticks of double dynamite all tied together by the leather belt he wore under that beautiful, black, silk suit he had on.

Now the time came. The Compare cried, "HERE'S THE MOMENT YOU'VE ALL BEEN WAITING FOR!! THE STAR OF THE EVENING!! THE

STAR OF THE CENTURY!! OTIS REDDING!!"

Otis strutted out on stage, and there was an instant of hushed disbelief as it became apparent that beyond all power of reasoning, this was real! It was all here before them!

We started his first song, *Day Tripper*, and the band, the audience, Otis and the six sticks of dynamite all went off together.

People were gnashing their teeth, crying, jumping up and down and rushing the stage like they were possessed! The cops actually had to drag them away like at an Elvis concert! I knew it could get ugly, very fast, and I was scared. If Otis was taken away to stage left, there'd be nothing between me and them! And they would certainly run us over.

We just played and prayed.

He did six songs that show, and the intensity just kept going up. No English artist had ever implored the Almighty to intervene in anything, let alone a love affair, and they were stupefied as Otis prayed, "GOOD GOD ALMIGHTY," time and time again, fist raised up in triumph! He took them from heaven to hell and back, over and over!

It all went by in a blur, and by the time he went off, the entire place was spent down to the last, red half-penny.

Sam and Dave were incredible, but what Otis did that night defies description or comment. You just had to be there.

We were jubilant to have done what we did and proud of the job our brains did under those circumstances. We sat down and stupidly drank our beer, panting, heads hanging down, shaking side to side.

I was completely spent at twenty-six years old. Andrew, myself, Duck, Steve and Otis were all twenty-six. We had the show of our lifetimes under our belts.

Only problem was, we had another one coming in less than two hours!

Now, I'm going to switch gears and move over to the trip diary I kept. I'll copy down a page, and if it's too sparse, I'll add some other memories of the day to flesh it out.

Saturday - *Upper Cut Club - two shows - owned by Billy Walker (middleweight champ of England)*

In addition...

Two shows again. It went well, and we remembered our lines better. But Otis kept the tempos fast. He seemed a bit hyper for some reason. Maybe because he and Jim Stewart had spoken about that very situation after opening night, and Otis had wound up telling Jim to stay the hell with the tape machines where he belonged. Jim claimed he was destroying the dance grooves.

"I came over here to do some shows," said a very upset Otis. "They're my shows, and I'll call the damned tempos. Those people out there don"t know nothing about no recording we're making! And I've got to entertain them."

It was very tense, but in the end, Jim backed down.

Sunday - *had a day off and went sightseeing*

In addition...

Steve, Jim, Otis, and Sam and Dave were not with us, but Eddie, Carla, Booker, Al Jackson, Duck, Joe and Andrew were. There were some others I don't remember. We had a bus and driver and were all excited to be out on the town. Duck and I had our cameras with us, and we snapped away, taking film of girls in mini-skirts, fountains and soot-blackened churches, all to our deep chagrin many years later. We both just pushed people out of the way. "Move over, Booker, I gotta get a picture of that red bus!"

In my personal hour and a half of Super 8 film, only eight minutes include the people I was with. Duck's tapes were about the same. When I think what we missed, I shudder!

Monday - *left by Caravelle jet Air France to Paris - arrived P.M.*

In addition...

We took a cab into town to the Le Grand Hotel, which sounds much grander that it was, believe me. It must cover a city block, and the hallways meander this way and that. And the room numbers don't follow one another. Like room 1119 might be next to 1140, and that next to 2033! It was like they had a code to keep anyone from finding their own room!

We finally got settled in and decided on room service and a walk around. Then early to bed, because we were so tired, and a long day awaited. Andrew tried first and couldn't get anybody in the kitchen to understand him, so he hung up and looked embarrassed. Then Joe picked up the old-fashioned, black phone and asked the hotel operator for room service. Once again, English would not do, and Joe hung up red-faced. I was getting a little mad, so I snatched up the thing and asked for the kitchen, determined to get our point across that we wanted three steak dinners. When the waiter began talking to me in French, I blurted out, "We wanna De steaks!"

It came out sounding like fake Italian.

Andrew laughed so hard he fell backward onto the ancient chair behind him, and it broke like matchsticks under his two-hundred pound plus frame! His ass hit the floor, and parts of the chair went flying everywhere. Joe and I fell onto the bed and cried with laughter for ten minutes. We finally quit and decided to hit the streets for something rather than go through this silliness anymore.

The first time in Paris can be shocking to homeboys like we were, and we had a ball with the menus and waiters. Laughing at everything so much that we had the restaurant crew laughing, too. It set the tone for the rest of our time there.

Tuesday - *Rehearsal in theater "Olympia" - 2 shows -*
Then press reception and buffet at theater
In addition...

Everyone was excited to be in Paris at the Olympia. The place was classically beautiful and old. No telling what had gone on there before, but surely many events of world importance. And here we were. Sold out in Paris, France!

On show day, there was no time for anything but work. We rehearsed in the afternoon and got ready for the recording. Once again, Tom Dowd had gotten hold of multi-track equipment and was ready to record the whole night. Everything was running smoother in the band as we got more confident in our stuff and our steps. The performers were as hot as they could get, but Jim was still concerned about the tempos. And we were uncertain about the outcome of the power struggle. Phil Walden, Otis' manager, figured into all this, but we didn't know how. We were pretty sure he was backing Otis and were secretly worried that the label might loose him. Atlantic could put him wherever he wanted to go, we figured. And even though everyone on the show was great, Otis was the force that drove it all home.

That night, the first show was stupendous! In the middle of Sam and

Dave's set, the audience jumped up and down so hard it looked as if the balconies (there were four) would actually fall. The theater manager was forced to come out on stage and stop the show until he could get them settled down enough to say he'd call it off unless they stopped jumping up and down.

It was totally frightening. I'd never actually been afraid on stage, except maybe during the hot dog fight at the Gator Bowl.

Finally, the show started back, and things went just fine until the end of the second show. Otis had them weeping, whipping their heads back and forth like crazed horses, gnashing their teeth and jumping up and down again. The manager walked back out on stage, but Otis wouldn't stop marching up and down. So the man just threw his hands up and walked off, talking to himself.

Afterwards, we had a reception downstairs with some food and drinks. Lots of excited talking and interviewing and more drinks. The press was hysterical over "black" music, and some of their eyes were glazed over at the white participation in it. I tried to explain that it was all of us together, but I don't think I really got that message over. It was not what they wanted to hear.

More drinks. Nice.

The next morning, Al Jackson and I had to have a doctor we were so sick. I mean commode hugging sick. I threw up so hard I lost my voice. The doctor said we'd had ice in our drinks and that probably gave us a stomach bug that would be this violent. We got shots and pills, for which we were grateful, and we learned a painful lesson about the water in Paris! Don't do it!

Wednesday - *Left Paris p.m. via Caravelle to London - then B.E.A. to Leeds, England - one show at Queens Hall*

In addition...

When we arrived at Paris' Charles de Gaulle airport to leave for London, we were getting into the spirit of the trip, and even though we hurt a little, hell, we didn't mind. We were anticipating more approval back in England and were ready to push on.

As we descended the steps from the bus, clothes bags hanging over our shoulders, one of our group who had purchased some hashish in Paris, was standing on the pavement trying to get rid of his supply before going through customs again. He held the pipe up to other guys' mouths as they passed, and some took a big puff. Then as I passed, the bowl came to MY mouth, and for some reason, I just took as big a puff as they all had. Now us Memphis lads weren't completely innocent of drugs and such, but I didn't even smoke pot and had never had hashish. I have no idea why I did that except to keep up with the "big" boys in the spirit of the occasion.

Suddenly, I was having tunnel vision and panicked feelings. I thought I'd never get through the airport like this, so I grabbed Andrew's coattail and stared at his back. "Don't go too fast, Love, I'm back here!"

And off we went. Me scurrying along behind and praying for deliverance. I remember insane cackling and snorting coming from somewhere close, and I vowed never to let those guys trick me again! I knew I was the laugh of the day, but I didn't mind, just as long as I didn't wind up in a French jail!

Thursday - *By bus to Manchester - checked in Piccadilly Hotel - two shows at Palace Theater*

In addition...

Nothing special except the two shows were taxing, because we were beginning to feel the effect of jet lag, excitement and fatigue. But we still had to kill!

Friday - *Day off in Manchester - bank holiday - everything closed - slept - played poker in Joe Gankin's room with the gang*

In addition...

Andrew, Joe and I ate in the hotel lobby and turned in early. I couldn't sleep though and read 'til late. Everything was turned around now with the clock.

Saturday - *By bus to Leicester - The Grand Hotel - one show at Gramby Hall - wild crowd - jumped on stage*

In addition...

If you've ever played on the stage and had a crowd "rush" you, then you know what it felt like that night. But in case you haven't had that particular experience, let me tell you!

There was a police barrier down front, and they linked arms to form a curtain. But when Otis was heating up, the crowd just couldn't stand it and rushed the stage. The screaming was at a fever pitch, when some of the girls actually got through the police. They jumped on stage and ran at Otis,

Wayne backstage with bus drivers

weeping and clawing at his suit and their own clothes! Security had to come out and drag Otis off to the side while the cops wrestled the women down to the floor and drug them sobbing back to their places in the audience. That they let the mayhem continue is remarkable to me. I really thought we were going to be run down like dogs and stomped or something!

Sunday - *To Liverpool by bus - did not check in hotel -*
two shows at Empire Theatre - first house was pitiful -
about 60 people (it's a blue collar town so people work late) -
second show was packed - great reception -
left after show for London on the bus - very cold
In addition...

We knocked them out! Then we were hustled onto the bus for a long drive back to London. We were not a very happy crew, because it was freezing cold on that bus. And we were feeling a little put out.

Monday - *Arrived London a.m. from Liverpool - slept most of day -*
two shows Monday night in Croydon
which is a suburb of London at Fairfield Hall -
Best two shows of tour to date -
Both houses packed - fantastic reception
In addition...

Monday was off in London, and in the afternoon, Andrew, Joe and I went down to King's Row to do some shopping. It's famous for men's clothing, and in one shop, I found a nice, leather coat I wanted. I got the salesman, and he helped me into it. He was very proper. My comment was, "Well, I love this coat, but the arms seem a little long." And he replied, without missing a beat, "Well, officially, sir, your arms are a little short!"

I'm surprised they didn't call the cops for reckless laughing that time. We're still laughing about it today. We ran out in the street holding our sides, but I still bought the coat.

Tuesday - *left Bristol, England by bus - approximately 150 miles - checked in at the Unicorn Hotel - two shows at local theater*

In addition...

The reception was terrific, and we did lots of press interviews afterward. We had some drinks to promote smiles on worn out faces and maybe some sleep. Worked for smiles, not sleep.

Wednesday - *Left for Glasgow by bus - all day drive - stayed overnight in Carlyle at the Crown and Miter Hotel - discovered crew misplaced my overcoat*

In addition...

We stayed up on a snow-covered mountain at the Scottish border, and the only heat they had was a huge, raging fire in the lobby. When I found out the room heat either didn't work or was non-existent, I just curled up in my clothes under the covers and tried to sleep.

Thursday - *left for Glasgow a.m. - Arrived 3 p.m. - checked in at airport hotel - went downtown to Paisley to shop - two shows that night at a huge dance hall - American sailors (ugh!) - Great show - three fights in crowd - played poker in the hotel resident's lounge 'til 2 a.m.*

In addition...

Great shows, but many fights, all involving American sailors and Scottish boys. They were during the shows, and we rooted for the locals since the sailors looked too drunk to win.

Friday - *Left Glasgow via B.A.C. turboprop for London - arrived 2 p.m. -*

Checked into Mayfair again and went shopping with Duck and Andy - one show at Round House - coldest, most miserable place I ever played, period - dressed in the bus in the parking lot because it was warmer - (Carla hung a blanket or something up in the back for a little privacy) - Everyone was sick with colds and sore throats - French and English TV networks filmed the show - Doctor came to the Mayfair at one o'clock tonight and checked everyone over - I got three medicines

In addition...

They seemed to help.

Saturday - *Phoned Bristol & found overcoat - they agreed to ship to Polydor Records - Left via train for Manchester where we got bus for Nelson, England - arrived Burnley in Lancashire County, England, on Saturday afternoon - one show at the Imperial Ballroom in Neslon (4 miles) - big success - leave at noon Sunday for Birmingham*

In addition...

I love the British. They know the importance of an overcoat!

We were a huge success. Somehow, we made it to a hotel and crashed until the next morning when we left for Birmingham, England, at noon, dragging our clothes and rumpled selves to the bus.

Sunday - *Rode with Noel to Birmingham in his car - through Bolton to Warrington in Lancaster County - noted for clipped accent, chop words - Arrived Birmingham Sunday p.m. - two shows at 6 p.m. and 8:30 p.m. - had drinks with Steve and Duck - went to bed and read*

In addition...

I rode to Birmingham with a man named Noel in his private car, just for the adventure of it. The countryside was so neat and beautiful. Noel ran a continuous commentary, so I think I learned a lot.

We arrived around two o'clock. We had two shows that night, and once again, the audience was bowled over and wouldn't stop cheering as we dismounted the stage. Was this what we could expect from now on? We were kids.

Monday - *Left 11 a.m. for Cardiff in Wales - saw Chipstow Carle and Cardiff Castle - one show at 8:30 - leave show for London airport -*

stayed over in Bristol - stayed at Unicorn again

In addition...

We saw Chipstow Carle (a fort) and Cardiff Castle (which gave me chills) and finally found the venue. We had trouble negotiating the skinny alley getting back to the load-in area. But the real problem came trying to understand the local version of English...Welsh. To a Southern ear, and indeed, ANY ear not reared in Wales, it is damn near impossible to understand. We stopped trying and got a local to listen for us. It was a good thing.

That night, everyone, but especially Otis, skipped over language and went straight for the hearts of the Welsh people with the most powerful transfer of personal yearning and pain, need of human dignity and love of his woman and country that I have ever witnessed, then or now. I saw this man reach out to people who may or may not have understood a word of his lyrics and crush them with his message. We were all done in by it! We had witnessed something. A transfer of information so sacred as to be unspeakable.

One show and like prophets from another dimension, we loaded up and proceeded to leave Wales for Bristol, where we stayed over at the Unicorn Hotel until dawn and then continued on to the hotel at the London airport.

Are you getting a feel for this experience?

Tuesday - *Left for London - saw White Horse Valley war monument - Roman burial mound - thatched roofed houses - Leave for Copenhagen this p.m. - arrived Copenhagen 7 p.m. - hotel 8:30 p.m. - bathed and went to Carousel Club - Good band*

In addition...

We all were pleased not to be playing. We, in the horns, could barely smile, even at a certified maiden, but we tried.

Wednesday - *Slept late - went to shop for souvenirs a little - sound tests for a radio show around 4 p.m. - press conference at 6 o'clock - first show at 7:30 - second at 10 - Smash! - went with Ron, Al, Steve and press rep to late dinner*

Thursday - *Lobby 8:30 a.m. - plane at 11:30 - arrived Stockholm,*

Wayne and Otis in the Stockholm airport

Sweden, about 2 p.m. - TV filming at club 4 p.m. - press conference at 6 p.m. - first show at 8 p.m. at Grand Halle Theater - Beer and sandwiches in lounge they kept open for us - Everything closed at 11:30 - slept like a rock until 8:30 a.m. Friday

In addition...

This next piece needs some reflection, so let me see how to continue. We were in Sweden and almost no one so far had spoken English to us.

We were all to be transported to the club for lighting, staging and cameras before two p.m. Outside the hotel were Sam and Dave, Andrew and I and Joe Arnold. I think we were actually late and a little nervous as TV is serious business.

The cab pulled up to the curb, and we all got in. Andrew in the front seat with the driver, and four of us in the back...me, Joe, Sam and Dave.

We cruised for a little while (the club wasn't far), and then Sam said quietly, "Hey, driver, you dumb, ain't cha?"

There were snickers.

Then Dave came in, "dumbest I ever seen."

A ripple of giggles.

Heckle and Jeckle had gone to work.

"IN FACT, I NEVER SEEN NOBODY SO DAMN STUPID IN MY LIFE EVER BEFORE!"

Open laughter bordering on hysteria.

Sam and Dave were off to the races now!

"You can NEVER tell when cabbies will be SO stupid they can't even find a place in their own hometown!"

"YEAH," answered Dave, "you can't EVER TELL!!!" They were screaming with unbridled hilarity. No turning back!

We came up to a curb, and the cabby pulled over to the sidewalk. He looked back at us with the calmest face and said in a nonchalant voice, "Now you guys want to go just down this alley here and into the second door on your right."

We all threw money at him and leapt from his cab, running down the alley, exploding with laughter and hoping he wasn't after us with a gun like he should have been. We were breathless with the enormity of the faux pas, but I don't think until now anybody has had the guts to tell it.

That night the concert hall was packed, and everyone was dressed in formal attire. They had come to see a concert.

We were all in place, and when the time came, the curtain rose. There was a scene of excitement as Booker T. and the MGs got started, and they rocked hard. When it was over, there was no applause. Just a rustling of faint whisperings. They were wearing white gloves, too. It was strange and unsettling.

Then the boys did their second number to the same response.

The Mar-Keys were announced, and out we strolled. The people were shifting around in their seats, making rustling sounds and smiling. At least, they were smiling! We went through our two songs, and the excitement seemed to be growing. A smattering of gloved hands patting together. Good grief!

Now, our "name" singers began coming out. Better response now. A hoot or cat call and some clapping. A yell! Lots of talking between songs.

We were all put off badly. We didn't know what to think, and nerves were frayed.

When Sam and Dave came out dancing, you could feel the charge in the air, and there was calling out and loud noises from the audience. Those guys were determined if I ever saw! The stage floor was a sea of shiny, slippery sweat when they left.

We started Otis' music and out he strutted with that huge smile and lifted his hands to the roof and shouted "GOOD GOD A'MIGHTY!"

The tension that was restraining the Swedes began breaking, and a mighty cheer went up. They remained seated though.

They quieted down again, and Otis gave it one hundred and ten percent. But I could tell he was disheartened a little as his set closed. He gave his deep bow and thanked them as we continued to blast *I Can't Turn You Loose* over his head. Finally, he left the stage, and we stopped the music and stood there while the curtain came down. I know we were all thinking the same thing. We came over here and laid the biggest, stinkingest egg that ever stunk up Stockholm and gotta do it again in a minute! Damn!

It was very quiet out in front of the curtain. Then, suddenly and unexpectedly, the curtain went back up, and as one, the audience rose, stripping off the white gloves and a deafening roar went up! Clapping like you never heard and screams of pleasure. Out of backstage ventured the cast with Otis in front, and it really got wild out there. They went bonkers and stayed that way, tears streaming down many faces, and some were pouring out into the aisles. Ten, twelve, fifteen minutes, it went on, until the ushers had to come and ask people to leave so the next crowd could come in. The curtain slowly lowered, and all the cast were shaking hands and laughing in amazement. All except the youngest of our troop and perhaps the most tender, Arthur Conley. He was weeping.

We had a new experience to digest. The Swedes had come to see a concert, and as anybody knows, you can't hear a concert if you are standing and yelling. They came dressed to honor the music and performers and did with restrained attention. Then in the end, they showed their appreciation. But, Oh God, did they put the fear in us!

The next show was much the same. At least, we were more relaxed.

When we got back to the hotel that night, we slept like rocks.

Friday - *8:30 call - Left for Oslo, Norway at 11:30 a.m. - arrived about 3 p.m. at hotel - fabulous scenery coming into city - bought luggage for Steve and myself - press conference at 4 p.m. - first show at 7:30 - second show at 10 p.m. - Smash again!*

In addition...

It was the most fabulous scenery coming into town including the Viking Museum, which we didn't get to stop at. One of the true disappointments of our trip.

That afternoon, Cropper and I went and bought additional luggage, Swedish leather, to carry stuff in, and we were very happy with our purchases.

The shows that night were the best. We'd been out long enough for all of us to just be natural. I think the best thing about them was the level of beauty among the young girls that were there. Young men's paradise! These girls rode bicycles everywhere, and their bodies reflected that! All we could do was gawk and swoon. Blondes and blondes and blondes. They really were as beautiful as the books said. And we were sure as free. But we couldn't stay. The next day was back to London. We were headed home soon, and none too soon!

Saturday - *Everyone happy to be in the lobby at 7:30 a.m. -*
Left for London via Copenhagen by prop and jet from there at 11:45 -
landing at London now at 2:30 - last two shows tonight at the
Hammersmith - leave as soon as possible after last show - Everyone happy
In addition...

Everybody was happy to know the tour was winding down. We took the prop jet to Copenhagen and the pure jet on over to London, landing at two-thirty p.m., then on over to the Mayfair for our last night. But that afternoon, something happened I am going to speak about.

I was sitting in the lobby watching the world go by when Otis came out of the elevator. He was dressed casually, whistling and singing to himself like he did, and he walked out into the driveway, or portico. Two big, black cars pulled up, and the driver got out and let Otis in the back. No big deal. Lots of people wanted to take Otis for a ride in London. But it felt funny. He didn't notice me, and I didn't acknowledge him either.

I went to my room and started packing a little, so it wouldn't be so frantic in the morning and then went back to the lobby for another cup of coffee and a final look around.

The cars that had borne Otis away came back up the drive and into the portico and stopped. The backdoor flew open, and the big man we all loved so much came tugging himself out of the back seat and slammed the heavy door behind him, not looking back at all! "Damn," was all I heard him say as he jolted through the lobby doors and stomped off to the elevators.

Rumors flew, and I don't know what to believe. But I know at the time, it was easy to imagine that the European Mafia was pushing him to be exclusively handled by them. I thought it might be true. And I knew Otis wouldn't have liked it one bit if anyone had tried to corral him like that.
So there I sat. And to this day, I don't know what happened. No more than you know now.

The Hammersmith Odeon Theater was packed for the last two performances. And I mean it was a fine send off, too! Standing room only for both shows, and I think the press had most of the tickets! We were a home run and didn't even know how big.

(I couldn't have guessed that twenty years down the road, I would be back on that same stage with another up and coming, young, black singer, Robert Cray, and we'd get an award for six, straight standing room only nights!)

After the tumult finally calmed down enough, we left the theater and packed up to go home.

To say we had a victory would make light of a very heavy world event, especially for Atlantic and Stax Records. And for Andrew Love and myself!

The rest of our lives were made, but we didn't know it yet.

God bless Estelle Axton, Jim Stewart, Chips Moman and Jerry Wexler.

Kings Of The Road

Andrew and Wayne c. 1967

After the stunning success of the Stax/Volt Revue, we were hotter than ever. And in addition to our frenetic studio pace, Andrew and I were doing gigs as The Mar-Keys, using various pickers for the rhythm section and Stacy Lane as vocalist.

We'd done this enough with different guys, until we could mix and match them and always have a good band. We were doing pretty well, too, going as far away as Fayetteville, Arkansas, and Knoxville, Tennessee, and we were getting enough money, usually through Don Dortch's International Booking Agency. We would pay all expenses, seventy-five dollars or even one hundred dollars per sideman and singer, and keep the rest for ourselves, maybe three to four hundred dollars each. That was nice weekend money! It doubled our weekly income from Stax in one night, and we had a good time nearly everywhere we went.

Except the time we played in my hometown.

Kenny Edmonson was my age and raised four houses down the street from me. Since ninth grade, he had affected a low, whiskey rough voice and smoked cigarettes. His daddy was in the Ramada Inn franchise business.

One day, I was in the club at the Ramada Inn in West Memphis to get a drink on my way home and ran into Mr. Edmonson. I hadn't seen him in years, so we began to catch up. He asked me if I'd like to do a couple of nights in the club to give the old friends in West Memphis a chance to see me. That sounded like a blast, and I said sure, why not. We decided on two nights, a Friday and Saturday, so everyone would get a chance to drop by. I was excited. The first time to play my hometown!

The next day I told Andrew about it, and he agreed. We called Marvel Thomas to play piano, Allen Jones to play bass, Michael Toles to play guitar, Joe Grey to play drums and Stacy Lane to sing. A great band. It was up tight and out of sight!

Our weekend finally came, and Friday night went as planned. We put on very good shows for my old friends and neighbors, relations and school chums, policemen and doctors I'd known since childhood. A lot of mother's friends came with their children that were my age. It was a joyful occasion, and everyone was looking forward to more of the same the next night.

Saturday night arrived, and the mood was jubilant. My brother, Bruce, was sitting at the end of the bar nearest the bandstand having a great time with the rest of the guests, including some of his old high school buddies from the football team.

We played our first set, which featured my first record, *Last Night*, and some more Stax instrumentals. The crowd was delighted and responsive, looking forward to more of the same in our last set of the night which was coming up.

We took our bows, and as the applause died down, I drifted out into the crowd and began greeting the people I knew and introducing Andrew around. Everyone was very complimentary and friendly. Then, I noticed a table with four guys waving for me to come over. They were obviously drunk and talking too loud. I recognized one of them as a bully I'd known in high school, the son of a local, well-to-do farmer. He was red-faced and leering as I walked over. I felt the redneck mean mood rising off him like swamp stink, and the hair went up on the back of my neck.

"Hey, Wayne," he yelled. "Hey Wayne, can your niggers play *I Didn't Know God Made Honky Tonk Angels*?"

What!? I couldn't believe my ears. I felt the silence spread around me and knew my face was flushing.

Even the bully's three friends were shocked at the look of stupid, pig-like hatred on his face. His lips curled down in an ugly mask of defiance. "I said," he shouted, "can your niggers play *I Didn't Know God Made Honky Tonk*

Angels?"

Marvel must have sensed trouble as seasoned night club players sometimes do, because at just that moment, he counted off the first number of the set, *Grazin' in the Grass*.

There was ice water in my gut, embarrassment and anger swelling up inside me. I turned to leave his table, and all I could think to say was, "Yeah, they can play anything you want to hear! In any key!"

As I got to my spot next to Andrew on the dance floor where we were performing, my knees began to wobble, and my mouth got dry. I tried to control myself as I put my horn to my lips and started the melody with Andrew. Then out of the corner of my eye, I saw the bully leave his table and start around the back of the room as though he was moving to try and get a better look at us. My skin was crawling as I lost sight of him around the left side of Andrew, but I blindly went on as though everything was all right.

Then the son-of-a-bitch did what I could have never dreamed. He came from the floor with a hay maker and blind-sided Andrew.

Andrew came crashing down behind me, falling through the horn stands, amplifiers and guitars like a felled tree. I raised my head and looked left to see a giant fist coming toward my face. I snatched my head back just in time to save a broken nose, but he connected hard with the back of my head, knocking me sprawling sideways under the table next to the dance floor where I banged my head and shoulder as I skidded to a stop. Thinking I'd have to ward off another attack, I rolled over on my left side.

But when I looked up, all I saw was my brother's sport coat as he flew over me on his way to kill the bully. Bruce hit that redneck so hard he skidded on his ass all the way across the dance floor backwards. It took all his buddies to hold Bruce off him. The bully was hurt bad, but Bruce wanted more. His feet churned while four, big men held him back. The bully didn't move to get up, which was the only smart thing he ever did.

Andrew had a big, angry knot under his left eye, and I had a goose egg on the back of my head. My vision was blurred, and I was stuttering. Friends gathered around to see if we needed an ambulance and offered quiet condolences as they sadly shook their heads and left.

The police were already there, but they had to send for an active car. I had a chance to think for a second even though my head was spinning. What the hell had just happened? Did I want to press charges? Hell yes. Andrew and

I were sitting at a table in the midst of the band and assorted management and friends with bar towels full of ice pressed onto our respective injuries. Everyone was mad as hell, indignant and in shock. Bruce just stared at the bully who stood there looking down saying nothing. He knew he was lucky Bruce was tethered.

After awhile, they arrested the bully, handcuffed him, put him in the squad car and drove him downtown to the station house on Broadway. It was only partly satisfying. I had lived in that town all my life, and I knew when a local farmer got arrested by local police for something like this, it meant very little. But to me, it meant a lot.

I was devastated.

A few days later, we all went to the West Memphis courthouse for the hearing. Andrew's brother, Roy, came to stand by him, and my brother, Bruce, came to stand by me. We fully expected another confrontation in the parking lot and were uptight until we got safely inside. Then we saw him. He had a bandage all over the side of his face and his other eye and lips were dark blue and badly swollen. He had taken a hell of a shot from Bruce, and I saw a smile flicker across Roy's face as he appraised the damage.

After Judge Rubens took the bench and dealt with some other drunk and disorderly cases, he called for us. We filed around the wooden fence and stood in a row in front of him. He shuffled the papers around on his desk for a minute, and then read the charges against the bully, noting that it was his third time in as many months to be hauled in front of his Honor for the same thing. He looked sternly down at him. We all looked sternly over at him, and the bully looked down at his feet. There was a pregnant pause, and then Judge Rubens said in a soft, nasal voice, "You look like you got the worse end of the stick. The next time, you'd better pick on somebody your own size."

And with a drop of his gavel, he fined him fifty dollars and gave him six months probation.

That was that.

We walked outside and stood around the parking lot for a few minutes kicking gravel to see if the bully and his lawyer would come out, but they didn't.

"I wish that muther would come on out and try some of this meat I got," said Roy.

Bruce said so too, but Andrew and I didn't say much. We were both wondering how many more bullies there were waiting out in the world that we'd have to face someday.

Finally, we all got in our cars.

I headed east on Broadway toward my house on McCauley and as I did, I searched the rear view mirror to see if there was a pick-up truck following too closely. I did that for a long time, until the chill left the back of my neck.

Even that incident in West Memphis didn't stop our mixed bag of skin tones and accents from running up and down the highway between Memphis, Nashville, Muscle Shoals, and Jackson, without a thought to the turmoil we might have generated in the last truck stop. We were all full of optimism, enthusiasm and youth, and we might have been invisible for all I know. I do know that for the most part we escaped real trouble. But close calls did happen.

One night, two carloads of us headed out to play a Mar-Keys gig down in Starkville, Mississippi, at the big fraternity party of the year. We were to open for The Bar-Kays. One car carried the drummer and keyboardist. In the other, my bright, red Riviera, I had what every Mississippi state trooper dreamed of, a slick-looking white driver, a black passenger, Andrew Love, a college Joe, Lynn Moore, and Tony O'Terry, a tall, skinny hippie complete with long, red, curly locks that hung in his face.

Since we were playing in a dry county at a college where there would be no alcohol, we stopped in Memphis and bought seven half pints of Old Forester, enough for each person in the band to have a drink before and after the gig. Stowing them all under the front seat, we commenced our drive down I-55 through both wet and dry counties in Mississippi on our way to work that night. It was early afternoon, and the mood was relaxed. Andrew was in the front seat next to me, Lynn behind him and Tony in the back seat behind me with his window down and that long, red hair flapping in the wind.

The speed limit was fifty-five in those days, and I believed it, especially considering my cargo. And I don't mean whiskey. Everyone was doing fifty-five, even the bus I wound up behind for a long time. We sat there and sat there at fifty-five, and before long a state squad car eased up behind me. After awhile, he pulled out and slowly passed me and the bus. He crawled around us at about fifty-seven, and I drifted on over behind him easing on up to about fifty-seven myself. Then the cop got over in front of the bus and slowed to fifty-five. There was nothing for me to do except go on around him for a little distance and pull over in front of him. It didn't suit him worth a damn, so he turned his blue lights on and pulled me over.

The cop took his time coming to my window. He was just sitting in his car talking on the radio, I guess checking out my license plate and giving me time to get nervous. Finally, he got out and sauntered up to my car, leaned down, took a long look in through the open window at all of us and took my offered driver's license. He studied it for a minute and then said, "Mr. Jackson, would you mind stepping out of your car, please?"

I opened my door and slowly got out. He had his hand on the butt of his service revolver, and I just wanted to be smooth. "Stand over there," he said, indicating the rear fender of the car. I moved backwards, and he leaned into the front seat not saying a word as he reached his hand under the driver's side. I heard the brown paper bags rustle as he began to extract the bottles. He straightened up and began putting the half-pints on the roof of the car, glancing at me as he did so. I began to turn as red as the Riviera.

Finally, he finished and turned to face me. "Would you put your hands on top of the vehicle?"

As I did, he patted me down. I was getting scared.

"Mr. Jackson, you may consider yourself under arrest in the state of Mississippi for the illegal possession and transportation of alcohol in a dry county. Follow me back to the courthouse, please."

"Yes, Sir," I said. I was going to be very nice and helpful. Then I heard a voice from the rear of the car say, "Well, you can tell we're in Mississippi."

It was what the cop had been waiting for, and his hand shot in through the back window, grabbed Tony by the collar and yanked him up against the glass so hard it busted his lip. His nose bent double, and his spectacles were smashed, shards of glass cutting his cheek but luckily not his eye.

"What did you say, Boy? What did you say?"

A sound came from Tony's mouth, but it wasn't a word. It was a gurgle. The cop shoved him back into the seat so hard it rocked the Buick. He gathered up the liquor bottles and stalked back to his squad car, depositing them in the trunk before getting in and making a squealing start for his little town.

We followed...an ashen driver, a bloody hippie and two shaken passengers. We all knew we were in for a very bad time.

"Damnit, Tony! What the hell did you do that for? Are you nuts?"

I was so rattled my mouth and throat were dry. I could hardly speak. I knew I had to keep my head, or we'd miss the gig and spend the whole weekend in jail. And in the Starkville jail, anything could happen. Oh, they'd only arrest me and maybe just kill Tony, but the rest would never get to Starkville on time. We'd also be sued by a fraternity full of guys with lawyers for dads!

I hoped the other car was still peacefully en route. Maybe they'd get there and do something that would make everything all right. I could dream couldn't I?

We neared the courthouse, and the cop was driving a little slower. Maybe he'd cooled off. We were all quiet again. I think the guys actually felt sorry for me, and I did, too.

We pulled up to the side of the white, wooden building in the shade of a huge oak tree and got out. The cop had his hands full with the bottles and his clipboard. He started around my car to get the license number, but before he went far, I darted around back of it and called the numbers off to him. He stopped and eyed me as he copied them down. "Follow me," he said.

The others sat very still in the car. They were being as small as they could be, and I think Andrew was willing himself white.

Inside, we stopped in a room with two doors, one marked "Office," the other marked "Judge's Chambers." He motioned me to a chair and said, "Sit there." His voice had lost some of its earlier edge, and I felt just a small bit of encouragement, but not much.

"Sir," I started, "we're just musicians on our way to play a fraternity party in Starkville tonight, and we got this liquor so we could all have a drink after the show. I'm very sorry this happened."

He looked down at the whiskey in his arms. "I see."

He disappeared into the Judge's Chambers and was gone a long time. The sweat was beginning to run from my armpits even in the air conditioning.

Finally, he came back in and stood in front of me shuffling papers for a minute before saying, "Well, we're gonna confiscate your whiskey and fine you fifty-five bucks for possession but drop the transportation. But let me tell you something friend, that son-of-a-bitch in the back seat like to have got you put away `til Monday!!"

"Yes, sir," I said as softly and heartfelt as I could while signing the paperwork he laid on the table. I fumbled in my pocket and came up with some folding money, fifty-five dollars, which I handed over. My mind was racing, could we make it?

"You seem like a nice enough guy. Now y'all git on outta here."

By the time I got in the car and my legs stopped shaking long enough to start the engine, it was five o'clock. We were cutting it close. It was all I could do not to floorboard it right back out to the expressway, but our patrolman was out cruising again. I didn't want to take any chances.

"There's that cop again," said Andrew lifting a half-pint bottle of Old Forester up to his lips and taking a long slow pull. He was smiling as he lowered the bottle and wiped his lips. "Aaaaaah!" he said.

"Daaaaamn!" I yelled.

He had somehow secreted one of the bottles away from the cop back on the highway.

That took some nerve, I had to admit.

Andrew and I were sharing experiences that bond people. We were also making pretty good money doing it, and it was dawning on both of us that together, we were stronger than apart.

The Summer Of Love

Meanwhile, the Otis Redding train steamed through the mountains and pastures of the rhythm and blues landscape, pulling carloads of musicians, writers, executives, press corp, and adoring fans as it went. It seemed that nothing could stop it. And certainly no one aboard would have stuck out a toe to slow its progress. Man, it was going fast, and it was headed home to Georgia.

The National Association of Recording Manufacturers was having a big convention in Atlanta and the whole Stax/Volt Revue was to perform. Then the next day, we would go to Macon for a huge barbecue at Otis' ranch, The Big O.

We stayed at the Hyatt Regency, the posh, new hotel in Atlanta. When we arrived, Jesse Jackson met us in the lobby. I don't know why he was there, but I didn't consider it a good omen. After being introduced to me he said, "Musta' been a Jackson in the wood pile, huh?" It was meant to be inflammatory. I was so embarrassed, but I just laughed, aiming my red face at the floor. I was glad when we broke up and went to our rooms to get ready for the evening's performance. My brother, Bruce, had come with me, and we were sharing a room. He had hit it off with Cropper and was excited to be hanging with him. We were all excited and talked about the possibilities for fun during the next two days.

The show that night was another huge success, the only glitch being that Dave Prater didn't show. There was general angst going on backstage over his whereabouts, until David Porter stepped up and said he would be glad to go in Dave's place. The announcer said that the songwriter of Sam & Dave's important hits was going to take the stage with Sam. The crowd ate it up, and David showed what a performer he really was. Otis shined especially bright since his family and friends were in the audience, and the band was ridiculously smashing! It was one hell of a performance.

Later that evening, Janis Joplin was playing at a local hot spot, and I went with Andrew to catch the show. When she finished her set, she came over to me and after introductions and a short conversation, asked me to be her bandleader! She wanted something from Otis, if it was just his trumpet player. God I was rattled! She was serious, and I just didn't know what to say. I didn't want to spoil the groove I was already in, so I mumbled some excuses and made my way back to the hotel.

The next morning, we went over to Otis' house on a Greyhound bus. Andrew and I and a cast of all black preachers, politicians, disk jockeys and who knows who else were on board. We sat in the third row seats, him by the window and me on the aisle. From grinning faces at the show and reception the night before, these guys turned into snarling nightmares, shouting, "white mad dogs!" as they stormed up and down the rocking bus aisle, slamming their fists on the back of all the seats. As the only white person on board, I shrunk down into my seat, trying to be as small and as close to Andrew as I could get, hoping they would stop the bus and set me off on the side of the road. But they didn't, and I suffered in quiet misery the rest of the way.

Finally, we arrived at the ranch. And when I saw Phil and Alan Walden a little ways off, I rushed over to be with other white faces, glad to have made it there without getting hurt. It was the first time in my life I had ever been intimidated by black people, and I was a little shook up. It dawned on me that the racial divide in the country was going to be very serious.

The delicious barbecue smoke wafted thick in the air, and even after my fright, I was getting hungry. First though, Otis came by with Jim Stewart in tow and cornered me. "Come on, Jackson, I wanna show you my house!"

Zelma appeared, and we all walked around the big "O" shaped swimming pool, oohing and ahhing at the majesty of it. Then on through the beautiful, dark wood farm house with the three-sided, wrap around porch. Otis pointed off towards a field where his favorite horse was eating grass. He loved to ride.

We went in, and Zelma seemed especially proud and radiant, beaming as she showed us her kitchen. She's a lovely woman and was very happy about Otis' success.

Now the mood was jubilant. No race talk or bad vibes. Just barbecue eating and beer drinking. Still, I hung as close to Alan and Phil as I could and tried to keep Andrew in sight in case there was a chance to get back into town. I was in a hurry to have some fun. We were supposed to meet up with Bruce and Steve back at the hotel, and I sure didn't want to miss anything. So I began asking about rides.

Finally, there was a car heading to Atlanta. I grabbed Andrew, and we fled the scene. We were back in control of the situation, whatever that was, but there'd be no more screaming demons.

Next morning, we all boarded a DC-9 for the short flight home and laughed and pretended to be scared by the black wreath hanging on the forward bulkhead, and the black clothing the stewardesses were wearing that day. Very eerie!

If we had only known how appropriate those symbols were for later that year, we would have really been shook up!

New things were on the horizon. Seemed like we jumped from one thing to another, and soon after we got home a fast ball came our way! The biggest concert in the history of rock and roll up to that point was to be held in Monterey, California. It was dubbed a festival, because it lasted longer than one day...The Monterey Pop Festival.

And they wanted Otis.

There was only one problem. Otis had disbanded his band so he could take some time off to have polyps removed from his ravaged vocal chords.

Solution?

Booker T. and the MGs and the Mar-Key horns.

Everybody agreed, and Jim gave us the time away from the studio to make the gig. Otis needed us, and we were going to be there. Period.

It had been a long time since I'd been to California, but I wasn't nervous. This was MY deal, not some old cowboy star's deal, and I was excited.

Andrew, Joe and I arrived in Monterey on Thursday evening and checked into the hotel. We had been allotted two rooms. Joe got the single, because Andrew and I knew we would be up late. We were always too excited to sleep and would drink and talk until the wee hours. It was our pattern.

This Thursday night was no different. We went to the corner Denny's for some dinner, then to a package store for a fifth of Old Forester and back to the hotel to see what was happening. Joe didn't drink, so a fifth would do.

Because of some recording dates at Willie Mitchell's studio, the three of us arrived a day behind the rest of the Stax contingent and didn't really know what was going on. We soon found out. It was easy to tell where the rest of the crew was. The doors were wide open to their rooms and loud voices issued forth, especially Duck's. You could hear him from the parking lot. It was a two-story motel with no elevator, so we walked up the steps to the second floor and found the rehearsal party.

Otis was presiding. "We gonna do it just like in England," he was saying.

"Same show for me. I don't care what y'all do, mine's the same if we get the time. Don't nobody know how much time we're gonna get yet. We'll find that out tomorrow."

"So," said Cropper, scotch in hand, "we'll come out and do two or three songs and then The Mar-Keys will do their two and then bring you on. That right?"

"Yeah," said Otis, "then me." He was striding up and down the room in his characteristic way like a caged lion and emitting charisma like a locomotive whistling through the night. He couldn't seem to help it. And nobody minded, because they were charged by it, just like the crowds that couldn't get enough, except we were within touching distance all the time. Otis was our driving force and spiritual leader. Even though the rest of us had some instrumental success on our own, Otis was our hero.

"What about the tempos?" asked Al. "In Europe, they were pretty darned fast."

"Just like that," answered Otis. "I wanna keep em' jumpin'. I don't wanna turn them loose." Everyone laughed.

Duck was always red-faced, but tonight, he was a little more red-faced. He held his scotch glass in both hands between his swaying knees. It sloshed around a bit. "Damned right," he bellowed in his usual conversational tone, "Keep em' rockin'. We're up against Jefferson Airplane and Hugh Masekela and all them other big acts and we gotta do it." He threw his head back and roared. Everyone followed suit. Otis was really prancing by this time and slapped everybody's hands.

"That's the spirit!" he yelled. "That's what we gonna do. We gonna do it to them right. We gotta, gotta, gotta," he ended, and people were slapping hands all over the room.

Loud talk and drinking followed, except for Otis, who didn't drink. He went to his room soon after that and told everyone as he left to be sure and get some sleep. Fat chance.

Joe Arnold was the only other one to leave before early morning. Everyone liked Joe, but he was a little different from the rest. Not standoffish, just quiet. And he didn't drink or smoke and sometimes felt odd. He had a shy smile and didn't talk much except when he played his tenor sax. Then he talked plenty. Enough to make Andrew work hard, and that was saying something, indeed.

"Well," said Steve, as the party began to wind down, "we won't know anything until we get over there tomorrow, so we probably should get some rest. They say there's one hell of big crowd over there." He shook his head from side to side and chuckled. "No telling what's going to happen."

And he was telling the truth! If any of us had known what it was going to be like, no amount of alcohol would have put us to sleep that night.

Andrew and I left and went to our room, which was just down the outside hallway. I opened the door while Andrew held the bottle up to the light to see what was left. He seemed satisfied and ambled into the room behind me, closing the door and sitting down on the first double bed, the one with his luggage on it.

"Well, Jackson," he said, spinning the top off the fifth with his thumb and letting it fly to the floor, "what do you think? I think we're in California having a ball is what I think," he said, offering the bottle to me. "Buddy, have a drink."

It was a standing joke between us that each would adopt the other's ethnic form of rural speech when we were alone, and we took great delight in it.

"Here's to us," I replied and tipped the whiskey bottle up, taking a big slug. "To hell with those guy's at Hernando's Hideaway. That's what I think. This right here is the big time, and I like it."

"Right on, little buddy, right on," Andrew laughed. "To hell with a bunch of them at the Rosewood Club, too. This is a lot better than fifteen dollars a night. I guarantee."

The space around the edges of the drapes was beginning to turn from black to slightly gray, and we were still sitting face to face passing the bottle back and forth and talking.

"I tell you, brother," I said, pulling my Beatle boots off, "we just hang in here like we're doing, and everything gonna be all right. Sessions are picking up and who knows how far Otis will go. And we keep The Mar-Keys dates, and we won't need those stinking clubs any longer. I tell you, we can do it."

"Yeah," said Love. "I know we can do it. I'd like to get it to where we wouldn't have to go to Muscle Shoals so much. That stuff is wearing us out."

"Don't worry, we're getting there. We just gotta hang in. If Sam the Sham can do it, we sure can," I said, rolling over on my back. "Man, I'm tired."

"Me too." Andrew turned off the lights.

This conversation was a daily and nightly thing with us, and we kept each other pumped up with it. It's what we did on long drives to Muscle Shoals. We left early in the morning, arrived at noon, did a five-hour session and drove back to Memphis so we could do a gig that night. Then we'd have to be back in at Stax studio at eleven a.m. to do another session.

We were making our way into some good money for that time and knew it, but we needed this talk of more and more success to keep us going. And talk we did.

Sodden sleep came swiftly to us that morning, but the eleven o'clock wake up call seemed instantaneous to Andrew. After only ten or twelve rings, he picked up the phone and said, "Uung."

Booker T's familiar voice was in his ear. "We're going to meet in the parking lot in one hour. See you then."

It was a slow moving group that assembled at noon to board the vans that would take us over to the venue just twenty minutes away. Otis, however, was his usual bubbling self, the only saving factor of the morning. He was rocking back and forth in his seat, humming to himself and looking like the perfect picture of what he was.

"I feel good!" he would say and small voices would come back. "Me too," or "Oh, my head."

But Otis didn't care. He was ready and knew it. He was always rockin' on ready!

The van came around the corner of the stadium, and we began to get glimpses of the crowd. There was a chicken wire fence between them and the area for the performers, but lots of people had gotten through or around it and were standing around trying to be "cool" or sitting on the tailgates of station wagons and other vans. Many of them smoked marijuana openly, and there were cops roaming around. It looked like nobody cared. Crazy! Cops, hippies and marijuana all mixed up together. Scary!

A hippie band was just coming off, and the stage crew was tearing their gear down. Booker T's stuff was going up next, and then we'd be on. The sun was setting, and so was the temperature. Just about dark the security beckoned us. It was time to mount the stage. We climbed up the iron steps behind a black curtain onto a wooden floored area. And there, in front of us stood the heroes of the Sixties, the Smothers Brothers!

"Welcome, Welcome!" they chorused while shaking our hands. They were so close to us and talking like they knew us. Holy gosh! These were the guys with their own weekly network show!

"It's getting colder," I moaned to Love. I had to constantly blow breath through my trumpet to keep it warm enough not to be flat when we started playing.

"I know it," he replied, blowing breath through his horn, too. We were jiggling up and down.

There was a lot of moving and huffing and pushing and loading going on for about thirty more minutes, and then the big lights went down.

Suddenly, Tommy Smothers was center stage with a big, white spot burning down on him. The crowd noise, which was a big, ole jagged buzz, smoothed itself down out of respect for him, and he said, "LADIES AND GENTLEMEN! THE NEXT PART OF OUR SHOW COMES FROM STAX RECORDS IN MEMPHIS, TENNESSEE!"

Some applause.

"WILL YOU PLEASE WELCOME THOSE GUYS WITH THE GREEN ONIONS...BOOKER T. AND THE MGS!"

The bright spot on the floor ran over to the Hammond organ and shone down on Booker T. Jones sitting there starting the opening refrain to *Green Onions*, gently rocking back and forth in a lime green, mohair suit and grinning! When Steve hit the familiar guitar lick, the entire stage lit up, revealing the whole band, and the crowd began to filter down towards the stage. There was a cordon of police about fifteen feet from the front of the stage, but the crowd seemed to not want to break through, just get closer, like moths to a flame.

Hippies in the Sixties were used to bands with long hair, in worn out jeans and funky shirts, smoking cigarettes and drinking beer on stage, just like they were doing in the audience. Everyone wore headbands.

When those green suits lit up the night, they were excited and curious.

They never expected that.

It reminded me of Europe, just with a much bigger, funkier crowd.

The MGs did their thing and killed. Then Tommy was back on stage and introduced us. We were scared but brave and came out in our electric blues with shiny, black boots. When the crowd heard the horns with the MGs, they recognized the ensemble and started dancing and getting louder. They loved us!

I looked off the stage to my right and saw a young girl holding a tiny infant in her arms and smoking a huge joint. Oh, well! She was standing next to a pup tent that looked like it was on fire, a cop in uniform right behind it enjoying the fumes.

Tommy returned when we finished and announced Otis.

We started his music, and Otis came flying out on stage with such energy I couldn't believe it. He started calling to the "love" crowd...he begged them to come with him, and he was irresistible! He stomped back and forth across the stage, and before long, everyone was with him, strutting and laughing and crying together. His tempos went higher and higher, until it was very hard to keep up the horn lines! We just had to fly, and we did. He wouldn't let up at all, and the emotions were tumultuous! The whole place was jumping up and down with him and screaming. Fifty-thousand strong. We kept dancing, and what seemed like an eternity later, it was over. And the crowd was insane.

Tommy was out there asking for calm and asking if anybody had ever seen anything like that in their lives.

We came off stage, and the soaked to the skin Otis had already been whisked away to the hotel to change and do a radio show. We were left to wander around and try not to catch our death of cold. Our teeth were chattering, but we wanted to see the crowd up close so we could tell about it when we got back home. We began to stroll about the grounds, feeling privileged with our little identification badges on our lapels. I know many people recognized us, how could they not with our electric suits. But nobody stopped us or bugged us in anyway. There were lots of food tents, and tents with tie-dye t-shirts and jade jewelry, but nothing more. We figured all the real stuff went on in those little personal tents, and we just walked on by, still not trusting the cops.

Soon the cold got us, and we went back over to the staging area and caught a van to the hotel. After a hot meal at Denny's, we headed to bed, completely exhausted, and we slept like bricks.

The next morning, Andrew and I took a rental car and headed north up the coastal highway to tour wine country. The exuberance from the night before was still with us as we joyfully tasted wine in as many wineries as we could find before making our way back to San Francisco.

It was getting dark by the time the traffic thickened, and we found ourselves in the city by the bay approaching the summit of Beacon Hill in a strange car with a back seat full of wine, drunk, looking for the Jack Tar Hotel.

The hill was almost straight up!

"Damnit, Love, I'm getting out!"

"Hell," Andrew yelled, "this thing might go over backwards."

We had never seen anything this steep that could be climbed, let alone driven up.

"Don't let it die," I cried.

"I'm trying not to!"

He was riding the gas and break together for all it was worth, and though it was cool out, he was sweating. "Ain't nothing like this in Memphis."

The Jack Tar looked mighty good when we finally made it there!

On the way to the airport the next day, I drove.

And now after the success of both Monterey and the Stax/Volt Revue, we felt our feet were firmly planted on a road we could follow for the rest of our lives. No more talk of opening a bait shop.

The Hit Factories

So here I was listening to myself all over the radio, on hit after hit, just as I had predicted that day at Grandma's. In addition to the regular work at Stax, I'd also been playing sessions at all the other local studios and down in Muscle Shoals, Alabama, for the past couple of years. And now, things were really picking up the pace.

Muscle Shoals was becoming a force unto itself, rivaling Stax. I'd been going down there to make records since 1964. In fact, it was in Muscle Shoals where I did my first session outside of Stax with Gene "Bowlegs" Miller.

Bowlegs was a five-foot ten, black man, rounder than most with a balding head and an infectious laugh that had a dirty smirk in it. You had to love Legs! In his thirties, he was a trumpet player/horn arranger/bandleader, and he had the Rick Hall account in Muscle Shoals at Fame Studio. It was the only account down there. Rick, like Jim Stewart, had switched from attempting country records to rhythm and blues records. He had some success, and how Bo got there, I don't know. But he did, and he began taking Andrew and Floyd Newman with him, and then me. He was as street smart as they come and realized I was not only a guy that could play high and pretty and relieve him of that worry, but I might become a heavy at Stax. And he might need me, so he began asking me to come along, too. I jumped at the opportunity to have some fun and make some more sessions.

We'd leave Memphis early, say around eight-thirty a.m., driving the two and a half hours to Muscle Shoals and then start recording around noon. Sometimes we'd leave about six and tear back to Memphis to get whoever had nine p.m. gigs to work on time.

It was always an adventure!

For instance, I'd usually be the only white guy in the car, and this could present some dilemmas. To get to Muscle Shoals from Memphis, you had to go through Corinth, Mississippi. Just before Corinth, there was a Dairy Queen sitting on the side of the highway. We'd be hungry about that time, so over we'd pull. The first time we did, we all began getting out of Legs' big, ole' two-door sedan. Andrew and Legs out of the front, and Floyd and me out of the back.

Just as I straightened up and looked at the Dairy Queen real close, I spotted the "colored window" around the side. I was shocked. I knew it was going to be an embarrassing situation. If I went to the "white window" at the front of the place, I'd piss off all my black friends. And if I went to the "colored window" around on the side, I'd piss off all the rednecks inside. That might lead to some real ugliness. So I just handed Andrew five dollars and said, "I'll have a cheeseburger and a chocolate shake. Would you mind bringin' mine back to the car with you?" I eased down into the back seat trying to be as little as possible. When I looked out at Legs and the guys, they were hanging on to each other to keep from falling down laughing.

That's the way we dealt with racial prejudice at that time. There was nothing else to be done, not even when the cops pulled Legs and his band over on the side of a dark, Mississippi two-lane highway at three a. m. on their way home from a gig and made them get out and play.

I remember one particular day the four of us were headed down to Rick's. Again, I was seated behind Bowlegs, who was driving his late model Chevy, and Floyd was in the back seat with me. Andrew was up front in the passenger's seat next to Bo. We were not yet to Corinth when the conversation turned to who had done the most for whom in the course of their lifetimes. It was between Bowlegs and Floyd. And because Andrew and I were too young to be involved, we just sat and listened, unable to comment.

"Yeah," said Floyd, in a pleasant enough tone, "if I hadn't started to college, I guess this would be MY gig we're goin' to now."

Bowlegs looked back over his shoulder at Floyd, and his eyes bulged out a little, "This here been MY gig since Rick started recording down here, man, whachu' talkin' bout'? I'm the one got chu' the gig with B.B. when you got home from the army!"

"Well, thanks, man, I didn't know that! I thought I got the gig, because I auditioned for it!" Floyd said, speaking with more exact English. "Besides that, YOU wouldn't be on NO Stax sessions, unless I said so! Ask Wayne!"

But I wasn't asked and remained silent.

"I been yo friend ever since we was kids, man," replied Bo, who was now looking over his shoulder almost constantly at Floyd, whose finger was up in the air trembling slightly.

Floyd was getting mad. "Well who started you off hominizin' in the first place?" His voice was loud now, and he reached up and touched Bo on the arm, which was resting on the back of the seat. Bo turned all the way around, reached over me and took a swipe at Floyd, "You BASTARD," he screeched!

"Hey," said Andrew, reaching for the steering wheel, "watch out!"

"Oh, yeah! You want to DO something about it," hollered Floyd, "WELL, PULL THIS STINKIN' CAR OVER, and GET OUT!"

The tension was horrible. "Come ON Bowlegs, DRIVE," I cried. And I meant it. I was scared silly by this display from two of my best friends, not to mention the danger.

But Bowlegs was not listening. He appeared to be in an absolute rage. His big, thick neck was bulging out and sweaty, and he glanced at the highway only occasionally. "You son-of-a-bitch," he finally screamed, pointing at Floyd's nose from the driver's seat, "I'll pull this car over all right!"

Andrew and I were scared to death!

"I'll beat cho' butt and STILL be yo' friend!"

That did it! The tension broke like a big balloon, and we all began to laugh. We laughed 'til we cried, and Bo was pushed all the way back from the steering wheel with stiff arms, head thrown back laughing. But at least he had his head going in the right direction!

Yes, the road to Muscle Shoals was bumpy but full of laughs, much like the times...too serious to be taken seriously, too funny not to laugh.

Now, Rick Hall, the producer, down there was a character. He sat in his swivel chair in the control room at Fame, long, brown hair falling down across his forehead into his large, liquid-brown eyes, with his tongue stuck into his cheek. He looked like he had an impacted wisdom tooth. It stayed there unless he was talking, which he did a lot.

In the early Sixties, we all had to be present to make a record. There were no overdubs, so you better get it right when you cut. God forbid, you were the cause of another take, and the reason for the loss of a great, vocal performance by a major artist! Say Wilson Pickett!

Rick kept four piano players on each session. Three sat out in the foyer, anxiously awaiting their turn, while the fourth worked on a song. If for some reason Rick didn't like what he was doing, he'd simply key the talk-back switch and say, "Next!" Then the hapless player would get up, slink out and tell the next victim to take over. They are all quite famous now...Spooner Oldham, Barry Beckett, Norbert Putnam, and David Briggs. But then, they were just in training. They learned a lot, however, it was a stinking pressure cooker. And a lot of sweating went on. Now days, they laugh and say what a great learning experience it was. You learned fast or you left. Simple. And we all learned.

Another reason I liked going to Rick's was the never-ending supply of dexamil capsules (amphetamine in the form of diet pills) that came from a quart jar he kept under the console in the control room. It was also fun to buy bootleg whiskey after dark from the drive-in window behind the local funeral home. It was so Southern.

Rick wanted us all to be happy like he was, so he didn't mind sharing his "stuff." I never slept. On the occasions when we stayed over, if I did get to go to the hotel, Rick would wind up sitting on the edge of my bed singing horn lines 'til three a.m. or so. I don't know how anything got done except for the iron will of Rick! But it did get done.

The local guys were at an advantage, because they had wives to go home to. So they did get some rest sometimes.

One day, we worked on a Wilson Pickett session at Rick's, and then Marlin Green called from his little studio over in Florence, Alabama, and asked if we could come by there on our way out to do a quick session for his new artist. Somebody called Percy Sledge that no one had heard of.

It was Bowlegs, Floyd, Andrew and me in the car that day, and we agreed to do it. We recorded a little ditty Percy said he'd been singing in the cotton patch with his family while picking cotton. We wound up with *When A Man Loves A Woman*! It's never been off the radio since the day it came out.

So in one day, we'd cut two major stars and one eternal hit! All in the span of an afternoon!

When that session was winding down, it was about five o'clock, and we had to rush out before even hearing a playback. If we had heard it, I would have surely asked for another take. Legs was just barely over the pitch on the long, descending line in the chorus, and I've had to live with that all these years...in the hotel elevator in Sydney, Australia, through the headphones on the plane going to Europe...just about anywhere I am, there IT is! Pitch problem! The horrible disease we just DON'T have.

So we tore out for Memphis and gigs. Then back at Stax the next morning at our usual eleven a.m. like nothing happened. Then maybe over to Willie Mitchell's place for an evening session. It went on and on, day after day, year after year.

The thing was we were making hit records down there, just like at Stax. Rick was developing a rhythm section that was beginning to get recognition around the world. Record companies were coming down to sleepy Muscle Shoals and liking what they saw. For one thing, it was self-contained. Everything you needed was local and cheap compared to New York or Los Angeles. As a bonus, and very important, the stars could work without their myriad of friends dropping by for who knows what. They could even stay at the Holiday Inn and eat at the Omen House across the street without being hassled. It was nothing to see Rod Stewart sitting there in the wee hours, all alone, eating scrambled eggs. Just him and the waitress. So stars were coming in and out of there.

Even Cher.

For that one, Dan Penn and I drove to Muscle Shoals in his new Cadillac and with the help of some little green amphetamines, stayed up five days. But in that time we wrote *Always David* with Eddie Hinton and had it recorded by Cher. That same week, Andrew and the guys drove down from Memphis, and we put horns on the whole album.

This was a solo album on her. Jerry Wexler and Tom Dowd were down from New York to produce, and Sonny was there. Jerry sat at the console by the engineer, Jimmy Johnson, and Sonny paraded around behind them in the small control room and peered out onto the floor over Jerry's shoulder, like he was fixing to give instructions. The horns gathered around the piano with Tom, working out the parts we would add to the music, while Jerry was making his opinion known via the talk-back system. We could see he was moving between Sonny and the control room mike occasionally, as often as Sonny seemed to have a verbal contribution to make.

We, on the floor, had our hands and minds full trying to remember what it was we were supposed to play, according to Tom, and making allowances for Jerry's "Manhattan" comments all the while. These guys were like cartoon characters to us country boys. They were SO New York!

We could tell Sonny was about to explode by the way his eyes bulged out of his head as he quick-marched along the back wall of the tiny space beyond the glass and by the numbers of times he lunged at the mike and got blocked by Jerry.

We were working on a counter-melody to Chers' vocal when Sonny could stand it no longer. He reached around Jerry's body, flipped the toggle switch to "talk" and said, "No, no, not that way. It should be more like an oom, pah, pah-oom, pah, pah, you know? Kinda like a German marching band thing! Try that."

Tom leaned his head down, putting the eraser of his pencil up to his forehead and slowly closed his eyes. Jerry now stood facing Sonny.

I looked at Andrew, and we knew that all of us understood what to do.

Floyd played, "OOM," and the rest of us followed with, "PAH, PAH!" We continued that until it sounded very much like a Viennese waltz played by a German marching band. It was hysterical. But there was stillness in the control room.

We grinned between pah-pah's and felt very clever until we looked up into the control room and saw Jerry and Sonny's heads bobbing up and down. They were pointing at each other's noses. Faster and faster.

Finally, Jerry put his hand on Sonny's back, and as they continued bobbing and pointing, propelled him toward the control room door, which led to a hallway and the door to the parking lot.

We could only hear them for a moment as they traversed the few feet between doors, but it sounded like two Yankee crows in a confined space fighting over a piece of corn. Then the parking lot door slammed shut, and we could hear the awful babble no more.

Tom shook his head and looked up. We were serious now, red-faced and hoping for time to pass quickly. What we had done jokingly was no joke. We were guilty of having a big star escorted from his own wife's recording session. I felt ashamed but more worried than anything. Would Jerry throw US off the session, too? Would they pull my song off the album?

I concentrated intently on how I should react, but my imagination was in the gravel lot outside.

When Jerry came back in and pulled the door shut behind him, we all heard the unmistakable "shoomp" of the thumb latch going home and knew the conversation was over. Sonny was on his way back to the Holiday Inn, but not before kicking a few toe fulls of gravel at the sky.

So there we were burning up the highway from Memphis to Muscle Shoals, sometimes two or three times a week. And we thrived on it! After the Stax/Volt Tour, Andrew and I were beginning to be a hot item at Atlantic Records, too. Jerry Wexler began calling us to come up to New York

Arif Mardin conducting, unknown sax player, Andrew, Wayne, Charlie Chalmers - Atlantic Records 1968

to do record dates on Aretha Franklin, King Curtis and others in the Atlantic stable.

He'd call me up and say, "Hey, Wayne, I need some of them 'Memphis Horns,' baby!"

That's where we got the idea of taking that name for ourselves and incorporating, although it didn't happen until later.

We would fly first class to New York on Thursday morning, get there at noon and check in the Holiday Inn on 57th Street. We'd work Thursday, Friday and Saturday. Then we'd get back on the plane Saturday night and come home. Although we had everything we needed in first class, we always carried a pint of Vodka in each of our briefcases, in case we ran into a big thunderstorm and they stopped serving. We pretended fear of flying in order to party on. Andrew and I always enabled each other.

While we were at the hotel, we could have steak and lobster, a bottle of wine apiece, champagne and cherries jubilee brought to the room. And we would get to sign the ticket! This was the first time anyone ever did this for us. That's what you do in the big time when there's plenty of money. Of course, back home, our own people cheaped us so badly that when the Jews in New York started treating us like humans or New York musicians, we loved it.

At Stax, we were used to buying our own bologna and hot souse (a meat-like substance so far beneath bologna, the package does not have the ingredients listed) with a Nehi, "big red bellywasher," next door at Jack's Number Two. At least the guy behind the meat counter gave you a free pack of soda crackers.

In New York, we were paid five union sessions at leader and contractor scale for every day we were away from home. That was about six hundred and fifty dollars per day in the Sixties, and my total layout per month was only two hundred and fifty dollars in a new, brick house with a new car. So we were bringing home about three grand each, plus they gave us lobster and wine at a great restaurant.

It was like a fantasy! Big time musicians like King Curtis were everywhere, and they would take us to Harlem. Somebody would have dope, and even though I didn't smoke dope, I'd have to take a big hit off of somebody's joint. Then I would be like Alice in Wonderland walking through Harlem with a bunch of black guys, going to jazz clubs and getting to see Clark Terry of "The Tonight Show" band and Yusef Lateef, a crazy saxophone player in the Village. We were traipsing around like we belonged! And I got tuned in to what New York City was about. There's no big time bigger than New York.

Then we'd go back home to the world of bologna and soda crackers where we were in and out of all the Memphis studios like figures in a cuckoo clock.

We were spending a lot of time at Sam Phillips' Recording Service. Charlie Chalmers was a talented saxophonist, songwriter and background singer, not to mention engineer, and he had a job over there kind of like Andrew and I had at Stax. He did that job, plus everything else he could get his hands on, too. He formed a vocal and writing group with the excellent guitarist and singer, Sandra Rhodes, of the Rhodes musical family. Boy, can she pick!

They, like us, were performing on everything. And he always called Legs, Andrew, Floyd and me to do horns with him.

Like the time Jerry Wexler sent Charlie a sixteen-track, two-inch tape in a heavy box, secured with electrical tape and wrapped in aluminum foil, containing his new Wilson Pickett single, "Funk Factory." Overdubbing had arrived by then, and Charlie was to produce the horns and background singers on it and send it back.

For this recording date, we were out on the floor, huddled around our familiar U-87 mike, and Charlie and his girl, Sandra, were in comfortable chairs in the control room.

Charlie put on the tape, and we began to listen so we could "hear" the parts as they became apparent. Charlie commented from time to time and gave suggestions. Then he'd back the tape up to the beginning and start again. It seems old-fashioned now, but that's the way we did it. And it worked.

Charlie was positioned so he could reach the machine, the console and Sandra at the same time. Their love was inspired and perpetuated by the music, and it was turned up loud. They kissed occasionally, and we were a little annoyed but said nothing. The creative juices were flowing, and for them, a little pot made the whole experience more enjoyable. We could see all this above the console through the control room window.

The smooching was into second gear by the time we got to punching in horn lines. Usually, Legs or I would give the cue when it was time to hit the button and the cut off when the horn line we were doing was finished.

Now, let me insert this. A sixteen-track recording machine has sixteen modules all stacked up neatly, and each module has a toggle switch that controls when a particular track is safe or armed to record. Only the track being used is supposed to be armed. The others are on safe.

We could clearly see the machine from our vantage point on the floor and were part of the failsafe system ourselves.

So we came to the place in the song where the horns would shine, and we figured out a line.

"Okay, Charlie," we said, "let's do this!"

Charlie rolled the big tape back a few feet to get a good starting point and sent it forward. The glass in the control room between us was about to steam over, but we could see them kissing as the crucial moment arrived. Charlie was still lip-locked with Sandra when he heard the last of the vocal verse pass. He reached back over his left shoulder and found the big, red "RECORD" button and depressed it!

WHAMO! All sixteen channels lit up as red as a fire engine!

Disaster!

We began dancing up and down, shouting, "Charlie, Charlie, CHARLIE! HEY LOOK!" We waved our hands frantically. Nothing like this had ever happened! In hysterical madness Legs leaned down into the U-87 and screamed in falsetto, "HEEEEEY LOOOOOK!"

And Charlie did.

When he realized what was happening, he nearly took Sandra's head off getting his arm free to reach the stop lever on the machine. He just stared up at the lights now gone back to neutral, and the color drained from his face.

We stood there with our horns hanging down and stared. None of us knew what to do or think.

It was silent.

No movement. It was ethereal and scary. I could see Charlie coming out of his cloud and beginning to assess the situation.

Finally, he turned to us and pressed the talk-back switch. "Y'all come on in and let's figure this out."

We went in, and he rolled the tape back. When he played it, there came a point where there was only a light hiss where there should have been roaring Wilson Pickett music. It was frightening.

"Okay. Okay...let's see here. What can I do?" It was obvious he was in shock.

Sandra was still and absolutely silent, gray as a ghost.

We were all aware that a career could be ending, and we all loved Charlie.

Because, as I said before, the Jews in New York, mainly Jerry Wexler, treated us better by far than our hometown people ever had. So you see the dynamic at work here in this moment of terror. We didn't know what Charlie was going to do, but we knew for sure there would be no more sessions winging their way down from New York. And there weren't.

We all ran for home like scared jackrabbits just as soon as Charlie gathered himself enough to let us go. The phone calls flew, but nobody ventured a guess as to the results.

What Charlie wound up doing was making a mix of the song down to a two-track machine that ran fifteen inches per second like a master. Then he took a razor blade and edited out by surgery the twelve bars where the horn solos should have been and sent that to New York for Jerry Wexler's approval!

I don't know if that record came out or in what form, but I'm pretty sure it wasn't the single. I heard much later that Jerry's verbal response was, "He put a razor on MY record?!"

We didn't hear from Charlie for awhile after that, but later, we did end up going to New York and Miami for all the rest of our work for Atlantic Records. The heat had blown over, and Charlie went, too.

Another hit factory was gearing up across town...American Studio. Chips Moman left Stax in or around 1963 over a dispute with Jim Stewart about money. Over the next few years, he cut a hit anytime he got broke and needed a new ski boat. That's why I attach the word genius to Chips and few others. If Chips had an artist to record and didn't have what he thought was a hit song, he'd just write one. Not just a song but a HIT song. And he did it time and again. That's a genius.

He'd cut a hit, send it to Atlantic Records, get his five thousand dollar advance and head for Florida, not to return until it was all gone and he owed everybody in both states. Then he'd do it again. It went on for years, until even the indestructible man was tired of it. That's when he came home and fixed up a little place in another ghetto at the corner of Chelsea and Thomas in North Memphis. The reason the studios always seemed to end up in bad neighborhoods was and still is simple. It's cheap!

American Studio was cheap but sounded great, and the all-white house band was to become the model of excellence. They didn't plan the all-white part. It just happened that way, because they all knew each other from giging in the white night clubs.

Mike Leech was the bass player who shared the spot with Tommy Cogbill, the great jazz guitarist who also played bass. Mike was an ex-trumpet player turned arranger, and he did lots of horn and string arrangements. He favored trombones and many times he hired the two trombonists, Jack Hale and Jackie Thomas. You can tell from Mike's body of work that he was very good at it. The soon to become legendary Reggie Young played guitar, and the solid in the pocket Gene Crisman was on drums. Bobby Wood wrote great songs and played keyboards. Earlier, he had regional hits himself on the Sun label, and while in pursuit of that career, he was in a terrible car wreck and lost an eye. They replaced it with a glass one, and it was hysterical when he'd take it out, lay it on the top of the piano and say, "I'll keep an eye out for ya!" Then keep right on picking, glass eye staring at the ceiling! Bobby Emmons wrote songs and played organ and other keyboards. His extra dry wit helped keep things light, too.

Charlie Chalmers and Sandra who were married by now, and Sandra's sister, Donna, were also there. They were Chalmers, Rhodes and Chalmers, and they did all the background vocals.

It's incredible the songs that came out of American and more incredible the songwriters! Aside from Chips himself with songs like *Born A Woman* by my fellow West Memphian, Sandy Posey, and many more, there was a stable of budding geniuses...Wayne Carson with *The Letter, Soul Deep, Neon Rainbow*, Dan Penn and Spooner Oldham with *Cry like a Baby, I'm Your Puppet*, Mark James with *Suspicious Minds, Moody Blue, Hooked on a Feeling.*

The artists were rolling through, and the guys just kept writing hits. These were golden days for songwriters. Write one at night and get it cut the next day on a major artist. Usually without a demo. I'm telling you, Chips' ears were THAT good!

Soon all the major labels sent their artists to American to record. Every kind of artist from B.J. Thomas to Paul Revere and the Raiders, Dionne Warwick to Neil Diamond. The excitement was constant, and Andrew and I were constant, too.

So that's what it was like for those of us working the studios...a baited field on the ground floor. And it was the beginning of the building process from which the Memphis Horns would later arise.

A Change Is Gonna' Come

In the midst of all this youthful wonder, making music history day after day and not even realizing it, the unimaginable happened.

It was December 10, 1967, and the phone rang just at dinner time.

Andrew said, "Have you been listening to the radio?"

"No."

"They're all gone."

"Who?"

"All of them, Otis and everybody. They went down in a lake."

We stood there on the phone for at least an hour remembering the last moments together and how it could have been us.

We were just silent for a long time.

Later, we would learn that Bar-Kays trumpet player, Ben Cauley, had survived. The only one who couldn't swim, Ben was thrown through the fuselage of the broken Beechcraft H-18 into the frigid waters. He somehow wound up with a seat cushion in his arms and hung on. He saw some of the others drowning but was powerless to help them and just grimly tried to live.

The line between Andrew and I softly hissed and crackled across the wide Mississippi that lay between us, and later we hung up, when our minds were as numb as Otis and them were dead.

And after what seemed like an eternity, the rest of our lives began.

But in my mind, I felt a darkness spread, and I knew a light had been extinguished that would never come back on.

It was an early, spring day that still had a little chill from winter in the air just four months since Otis had been taken. One of those brilliant, blue days where you could smell spring and feel winter when you walked.

Bowlegs, Floyd, Andrew and I had gotten a call from Charlie, and we convened at Sam Phillips' Recording Service on Madison Avenue to do his musical bidding.

The song was written by Charlie and Sandra, and they were cutting it on a black blues singer from Mississippi. I forget his name, but they had discovered him and thought he was hot. So they were spending their time and money on him.

As usual under these circumstances, we were all out on the floor gathered around the mike, and Charlie and Sandra were in the control booth directing and recording the session. The tracks were done except for the horns, and we marveled at Sandra's guitar and bass playing. She was so funky and slick with it. Wow! I don't know who the drummer was, but "Hollywood" from the Amazing Rhythm Aces was on B-3 organ. Man, what a sound! We were really grooving to the music and the fine talent and doing our regular thing by putting little stabs around the vocal and underlines on the four and five chords, staying out of the way. Once in awhile, someone would be clever and find a counter-melody that would make the whole thing tighter and more rememberable. We weren't really listening to the lyrics, but all of a sudden, I needed a vocal cue to know where to come in every time. So I began to listen for one.

And got tickled!

The lyric the soulful black man was singing went like this...

"MY BABY WEAR FINE CLOTHES."

Music...

"SHE READY FO' DE' ROAD."

Music...

"AND MONEY WON'T BUY HER OR GOLD!"

Music...

Well, I managed to continue playing but waved the others to listen the next time the music stopped for a playback.

They did, and pandemonium broke out. We all knew each other's sense of humor well, and since the singer wasn't there, we just cut loose! We all began jumping up and down and whooping and saying the phrases over and over again!

"My baby wear fine clothes! MY BABY WEAR FINE CLOTHES!! MY BABY WEAR FINE CLOTHES!!!"

Choking and slapping hands, and if you've never had your hand slapped by Floyd Newman, you better leave it hanging loose, or it'll wind up behind your back! We were wild!

Then Charlie came on the talk-back. "Hey! What's going ON out there?"

He knew us and figured something had struck us as funny. He loved to laugh, too.

Floyd got out, "Nothin' man. We're just giggly!"

We put down our horns and trooped through the airlock of giant, heavy doors, across the hall to the break room, just a small, windowless room with a couch, two chairs and a coffee table laden with Billboard magazines and a giant ashtray. There was also an "honors" candy box where you voluntarily put your quarter in and took one piece of candy out. I wonder how the accounting went on that.

Andrew, Legs and I lit up Marlboros, and Floyd waved smoke out of his face, still chuckling over the last song.

We had enough time to make a phone call each before Charlie stuck his head in and said, "Okay, let's do another one."

So back across the hall and through the sound lock to our horns and U-87.

We got in place and began to listen to the tape of the song Charlie wanted to do next. It was much hipper, and we began to groove with it, humming softly to each other and bobbing our heads up and down in trance-like fashion.

I glanced up into the control booth and saw the little, white phone light begin to flicker, indicating an incoming call. Charlie stopped the machine and picked up the receiver. He listened for a moment, and his chin dropped to his chest. He slowly hung up the hand piece and paused for long enough to get our curiosity up. When he spoke, it was too somber for Charlie.

He simply said, "Dr. Martin Luther King has been shot and killed at the Lorraine Motel."

I'm sure there was a visible shock wave that rippled our clothes, but we didn't see it.

Nobody spoke. We were inside thick, concrete walls, so we couldn't hear outside noise. Or I'm sure we'd have heard the city take a deep breath and sigh. And they couldn't hear inside, or they'd have been shocked by the scene in Sam Phillips Recording Service. We all drooped, knowing somehow that the world was suddenly altered never to be the same again. With lowered heads and pursed lips, we didn't say words but looked at each other in shock and then slowly began to walk over to our horn cases and pack them up.

Charlie did not speak either. This day was over, and we feared for our city, each from his own perspective. Three black guys and two white.

We filed out of the studio to our cars that were parked at the curb and stowed our gear in the trunks. I caught Andrew's eyes and said, "Wow. I'm going home and load my guns. I'll call you later."

His eyes were wet when he answered, "Me, too."

I pulled away from the curb and turned on the radio as I headed west towards town, wondering if I'd make it across the bridge without a brick or bottle coming through the windshield. Or even a bullet.

It was spooky on the streets, as though mysterious forces were gathering their strength to come swooping down from the sky. Still and quiet. No wind. An occasional siren was all I heard.

I made it home to West Memphis and went to the closet where I kept two 30/30 Winchesters and ammo and the two twenty-two caliber pistols Andrew and I liked to target shoot with. I loaded them all. Then I went into the living room, opened the front door and sat down. I hoped to have another garden out back this summer. Now what on earth made me think of that? It was like the old West but for real. Damn, I was scared.

Occasionally, I'd walk outside and peer off in the direction of Memphis to see if there was a red glow in the sky, then return to my couch. Linda and the kids were sleeping through the night.

I'd be ready if they came.

Otis and Dr. King may have been gone, but we knew we had to continue. Musicians are cousins by music anyway, and white and black knew we had to get along to live. And hell, we were simply having too much fun.

But still, change was afoot. It was even rattling its way into music.

And that certainly was the case over in the ghetto at American Studio, where Elvis Presley was about to alter the course of his career.

The electricity in the air was such that you could have cut the main power supply to the studio, and the machines would have kept running on their own. Elvis' personal magnetism had the paper clips flying off the receptionist's desk out front and sticking to the interior walls. Chips Moman was producing Elvis' first Memphis recording session since his days at Sun, and although we had been working on some pretty impressive artists, like Aretha Franklin and B. J. Thomas, everybody was sitting around with fixed grins or walking too much and bumping into furniture.

Elvis had his whole entourage with him, Red, Charlie, and Chief, plus a technical crew from RCA Records Nashville, an assistant engineer and engineer Joe Pechie, so the control room was hot and thick with bodies. And since everybody smoked in those days, smoke.

I arrived early for the horn date so I could be at the tracking session, and after nosing the Riviera around the crowded parking lot, settled for a space on the street, which was unusual. Then I walked through the backdoor from the parking lot and into the actual recording room where everyone was sitting, ready to play. Elvis was in the tiny, vocal booth in the left-hand corner of the room with his headphones down around his neck and answered my wave with a grin and the standard, "Hey, man."

I made my way across the floor, slapping hands and exchanging greetings with Reggie, Bobby, Mike, and Gene, the guys in Chips' rhythm section. Then I went through the door to the hall that was beside the control room.

Now the control room at American was about the size of an average living room in a subdivision home, capable of holding six or eight people comfortably. But on this day, it looked like a cocktail party at the Governor's mansion. I had to shoulder my way through the crowd up to the console where Chips was sitting, looking fidgety and chain smoking Camels one after the other. The German Shepherd curled up at his feet was the only one besides himself that wasn't talking.

"Hey, Wayne," he said. "Why don't you and the rest of the guys hang out upstairs. It's getting a little busy down here. I'll call you when we're ready for you."

He hadn't noticed I was the only horn there.

"Sure Chips," I said. "We'll be here." I squeezed my way out and down the hall to the reception room where another crowd had gathered and was admiring Ima, Chips' blonde, bombshell secretary, who sat behind the desk answering the phone non-stop and twirling her pencil. She was good looking and loved attention, so everyone was having fun.

You had to go outside the studio and to the right, then down an alley to the stairs that went up to the rooms that Chips had rented above the restaurant on the corner for his office and writing rooms. That's where we all waited for the call to come down and play. There were three small rooms, an L-shaped hallway with chairs and a table and the larger room where Chips had his office and a couch. A big comfortable couch I might add.

When I reached the platform at the top of the stairs, I could hear excited voices and the familiar call for "bucks up" from a poker game already in progress in one of the rooms. Everybody knew it was going to be a long night and had settled down to enjoy it. I had seen the "Doc" the day before and knew that me and the rest of the horn players wouldn't be too worried about the hours or how late it got. We'd probably be going through the next day sometime, and the whole thing could take weeks.

Meanwhile downstairs....

Elvis was a born cutup and enjoyed staying on mike while the players worked out the rhythm track for him to sing over. He would keep everyone laughing by singing the wrong and sometimes off-color words.

The gang that hung around Elvis was known as the Memphis Mafia, and it was headed up by Red West. He was there along with Chief, Charlie Hodge and Felton Jarvis. Felton had produced some of Elvis' records in Nashville and Los Angeles. They were all vying for the King's attention and making suggestions and prancing around the control room when Chips finally had had enough.

It was around ten p.m., and I had taken a break from the "cards and conversation" to come downstairs and see if we were close to being needed. I was standing in the outer office talking to Ima when I noticed it was very quiet.

I went into the control room, and to my surprise, everyone was standing around looking at the floor. Chips had turned the big, round, master gain control knob all the way off and signaled the number two engineer from RCA Nashville, to shut down the tape machine. He was red-faced when he stood up from his swivel chair and stuffed his hands deep into his blue jean, bib overall pockets. He surveyed the mob around him with a peculiar, little smile spreading across his face and with as cool a voice as he could muster said, "Something's got to give here, boys. I can't make records like this. Either I produce this session or you do. But somebody's got to go! You all figure it out and let me know."

He stepped down from the little platform that the control board sat on, pushed his way through the stunned crowd, strolled out of the control room and went onto the floor and began talking and gesturing to Reggie Young.

Felton Jarvis' face had gone crimson. He couldn't believe his ears. This was unheard of. A producer walking off an Elvis Presley session! No way! But it had happened.

I personally could believe it, because I had known Chips a long time and seen similar situations occur. Chips invariably won. But this was different.

It was E.

Elvis was talking to the background singers and was unaware that anything was going on when Felton depressed the talk button on the console and asked him to come in for a minute.

I backed into the dark corner under one of the big main speakers and tried to become invisible. I wanted to see this.

Elvis was having a great time, and when he entered the control room, he was smiling and made a joke about the great ass on Sandra. There was a little polite laughter, except for Felton, who was slightly stooped over and looking down.

"Listen E," he said quietly, standing to his full six-foot-one so he could look Elvis in the eye. "We seem to be having a little problem here with Chips," he said and cleared his throat. I imagine if he hadn't been in shock he would have shooed everyone from the control room before he asked Elvis in. "He thinks that it's been a little loud in here. He wants us to all leave, or he says he's going to."

The two RCA engineers were looking at each other with something like terror in their eyes.

Elvis was quiet for a minute. He took a long toke on his big stoggie, blowing a cloud of blue smoke up at the ceiling and looked around at everyone there as if to see what they were really thinking. Everyone was stock still, waiting to see if the King would blow. But soon he broke out in a big grin and put his arm around Felton's shoulders, squeezing him up close. "Listen man," he said softly. "I really like the way this is going. Chips is doing a great job, and it's the greatest bunch of musicians I've ever been around. So let's do this thing his way and keep it going. This song, *In the Ghetto*, it's the best thing I've had my hands on in a long time, and I can't wait to sing it. Why don't you boys just go on out to the house and leave Red here with me. I'll bring the tapes with me when I come home so we can all have a listen. But right now don't break my groove, man! I need to be working, so let's get it on here."

And that was that.

The bell rang, and Chips won by a knock out. Felton and the boys didn't waste any time either. Once the boss had spoken, they picked up their stuff and walked out, filing fast past Chips and making small apologies while they shook hands, mumbling to the musicians as they headed for the parking lot and the waiting limousines. In no time, they were out the back door and gone.

Chips had not returned, and suddenly, I was all alone in the control room with Elvis.

It was a little awkward in light of what just happened. But I felt as though I had to say something, so I tried to be as up as possible. "This stuff sure is sounding good, Elvis. That Ghetto song is a smash."

"Yeah man, I really like it, too. Wha' cha' been doing with yourself lately? I haven't seen you in years."

"Oh, remember that gig Charlie got me with Jimmy Wakley that time out at your house? I did it for a while and learned a lot, man, mainly to stay away from country swing music!"

Elvis waved his cigar and laughed. "I wondered about that, man. You looked a little green around the gills when Charlie said you were hired that night! I always thought of you as a rocker, but Charlie said you needed the job, so what the heck!" He was relaxing more now and enjoying himself. I told him some of the story of Jimmy firing me and Hershel Witt saving me. He laughed again. "Man, you done been through the mill!"

"You ain't lyin'," I replied, slipping easily into slang with him, the way I did with Andrew. "They done ate me up and spit me out, man, but now I can sho' nuff play *Love Song Of The Waterfall* with the best of em'!!"

He loved that and bent over laughing, slapping his thigh with the hand holding the smoking cigar. "Well, Wayne, I'm glad you're back here now, so you can play on my record! What else is new?" He had straightened up and was pulling his shirt down, so I knew he was about ready to go back to work.

"Andrew and I have been working our asses off and having a ball at it. We're on somebody's session about every day. We're still doing The Mar-Keys thing, too, and playing a lot at Stax, Hi and here. Chips is putting out the hits, man."

"Yeah," he said. "That's why I'm here. I could use one of those myself. By the way, wasn't that your wife with you that night?"

"Yeah," I replied.

"Not bad," he said, flicking ash off his shiny, black pants as he walked out to go talk to Chips, who by this time had settled down and was laughing and holding court among the musicians.

I whistled softly to myself and went out front. Ima was sitting there with a blank expression on her face, drumming her pencil on the desk and shaking her head. “I don’t know how he does it,” she said, looking up through pinched eyes. “I thought he’d really done it this time!”

“It’s hard to believe,” was my reply, and I left and went upstairs to spread the news to the gang.

Meanwhile, Elvis was singing the hell out of *In the Ghetto* and launching his career into the newest and highest phase it would ever go to.

We put horns on a bunch of songs that month, some with Elvis there and some without. Some while he sang and some we overdubbed. All with a lot of love and pride, and Elvis Aaron Presley was a happy man for a time.

Goodbye

Saying goodbye is hard. Whether it's to childhood friends or places where you learned or things you loved and have outgrown. So it was with Stax. That warm and fuzzy place where we were allowed to smile all the time like children and never face the fact that the world outside was moving on. Never mind the contribution we made to it in its passing.

It was 1969. Gulf and Western bought Stax, and when the suits from L.A. showed up, the fun was over. Along with their time clock and time cards came a work sheet. You picked one up from Linda Andrews at the front desk. She was Jim Stewart's girl Friday and knew more about the company than anyone. Then during the day, you had to fill in the eight slots for the eight hours of your time. We knew that this was corporate nonsense, and at the end of the week, some guy in Los Angeles would look these over and evaluate how efficiently we were being creative.

In response to this, we filled out the work sheets in this fashion.

Eleven a.m. - gathered at Slim Jenkin's Joint for morning beer.

Twelve - ordered cheeseburger and fries with second beer.

One p.m. - wander into studio to see if MGs have arrived. If so, inquire if our services will be needed immediately.

Two p.m. - make decision on recording.

Three p.m. - stand on sidewalk and talk to the Mad Lads about how high school is going.

Four p.m. - Slim Jenkin's Joint for afternoon beer and conference about nightly gig.

Five p.m. - turn in work sheet.

This is how ridiculous the corporate world appeared to us and how damaging it could be to the creative soul. We knew how much we would anger Jim Stewart and how much havoc it would cause out on the West Coast. But we didn't care. We just plain hated it. It was a real signal that the happy days at Stax were over.

And along about this time, three members of the local chapter of the Black Panthers came into Jim Stewart's office one afternoon and made him a proposition... "Pay us fifty thousand dollars by next week, or we'll kill you."

They left a ghostly white, red-headed Stewart shakily trying to get up from behind his desk and find Al Bell, his executive vice president.

Al knew the answer to Jim's dilemma and called Luther Ingram to get a phone number.

The two torpedoes he beckoned from New York City came streaking down south like a pair of grinning Great White Sharks, Dino and "Boom Boom." There was no mistaking who or what they were when they arrived. Even us small city guys knew they were gangsters, pure and simple. They were dressed like guys from the New Yorker Magazine. Dino had on a beautifully, tailored, striped wool suit with a crisp, white shirt and matching tie. Boom Boom wore a long, black, leather overcoat with leather hat and carried a black, leather briefcase. Dino was tall and nice looking with a believable smile, but Boom Boom was short and stocky with little, pig eyes and a wide flat nose, shiny like waxed mahogany. When he smiled, it was just a dark hole in his face.

Al Bell greeted them like old friends and took them back to his office. There, they were promised the position of head of Stax Security if they would do this one job for Al Bell. Get the Black Panthers off Jim Stewart's back and away from Stax altogether, forever!

That was simple enough. There was enough intimidation power between these two to hold off the National Guard on full alert! These Black Panther kids were just that...kids. Imitating their heroes and bidding for some of that Stax gold in the only way they knew. Extortion and terror.

Dino and Boom Boom went over to the old, run-down house the Black Panthers called headquarters and just walked in. Dino stood at the door while Boom Boom smiled his morbid smile, went over to the dusty topped plank they used as a desk and gently lay his briefcase down face up, handle and shiny thumb latches to him. He let the latches snap as he opened them up and lay the freshly cleaned and still oily 357 magnum it contained down on the plank. The giant gun would surely leave a print in the dust they could remember him by. He then spoke the only words spoken there that day.

There was no sound whatsoever from the young Panthers, frozen in time with bulging eyes.

"My friend and I now work for Stax Records. If I see your faces ever again in my life, I will kill you."

He lovingly picked up his piece and returned it to its house, closed the lid and turned to leave, his heavy coat stirring the air in the musty room, their place in the history of the decline of Stax Records thereby secured.

By that time Andrew and I felt really bad about the place. Nobody smiled anymore. Only the ones left making the "big" money, and of course, they were happy, happy, happy ALL the time.

But we were no longer included in anything except frightened looks and a whispered word here and there.

This particular day, the tension in the air was palpable. Andrew and I were standing around the studio floor waiting for something to happen recording wise, or else we were going to do our two p.m. getaway and just leave, figuring nobody would know the difference anyway. It seemed like a ship without a rudder. Booker had already made his exit and left for California. Steve was fixing to do the same.

Things were in disarray. Isaac was growing so fast they couldn't count the money, let alone figure out how to split it up. His lust for life and women became legend as he toured around the country in his custom coach, hiring entire symphonies in most cities and shocking patrons with his chained, half-naked performances.

All hell was breaking loose as people who would never have been let into Stax began to jockey for positions on the carcass. The place was full of people we'd never seen, and they were all titled with secretaries.

Andrew said to me, "Let's go out to the car, man. I gotta talk to you." Coming from Love, it seemed urgent.

We went out to his new, yellow Cadillac and climbed in. It had white leather interior, my personal favorite.

We were sitting in the back parking lot of Stax within the confines of the nine-foot hurricane fence with the "home for the criminally insane" barbed wire across the top. It was early September, and the sun shone hotly through the windshield. We were both sweating from our foreheads, and Andrew reached under the front seat and pulled out a half-pint of Old Forester.

"Man, it's only three o'clock," I said. "I gotta work tonight."

Andrew's thumb spun the bottle top on the half-pint so hard it flew to the ceiling and fell back down on the seat between us.

"Buddy, have a drink," he said, and took a long pull himself before handing me the bottle.

Andrew made a swig of hot whiskey look like a mouthful of cool soda pop. I could seldom refuse and didn't this time.

So I took a big gulp and after nearly puking, handed it back to him. He was wiping his lips with the back of his hand and gazing off into space when he casually said, "They're saying Boom Boom pulled a gun on David Porter last night and told him he would kill him if he didn't stop hangin' around Isaac."

The words were like thunder on a clear afternoon. I shrunk down in the plush seat as if to hide and put my hand over my face. "Damn," was all I could manage.

Andrew took another drink and passed the bottle. This time I didn't even sputter.

"Those guys are really crazy. I knew something like this was going to happen. You could cut the tension with a knife in there today."

"Yeah," said Andrew, "they say David's all shook up and don't know what to do."

"Me too! I don't wanna get killed just for hangin' around an old buddy!"

"Well," said Andrew, "if ever there was a chance to quit, this is IT!"

Here we were sitting in a hot car, drinking hot eighty proof, too scared for the alcohol to have any effect.

I took a deep breath and steadied myself. "Well, now's the time! Jim's in his office, and it's payday. You ready?"

"Naw, man, you go do it. I'll wait for you here."

He always let me do the fun stuff!

I had the strangest mix of feelings as I walked up to Jim Stewart's office...a little nervous but, underneath, a little excited, too.

I knocked politely, and he said, "Come on in, Wayne," looking up over the stack of papers on his desk. "How ya doin'?"

He won't let this be easy, I thought. He'll have to be nice. He looked a little gaunt, normally bright eyes darkly underlined.

"Jim," I said, "I think Andrew and I would like to go off the payroll."

Jim looked back down and said in his high, reedy voice, "Well, I was expecting that."

"Not that we don't want to do sessions here anymore. It's just that we can't go along with not playing anywhere but here. We're doing so good with Atlantic and over at Chip's place and at Hi with Willie. We want to pursue our careers in that direction. Hope you understand."

He held no reproach for me in his eyes when he looked back up and handed me two identical envelopes with the seal of Stax Records in the upper lefthand corner.

"Well," he said, "here's your last checks, then, and good luck to y'all."

I thanked him, and he said one more thing that would be true, "We'll be seein' you around the place, I guess."

"Yes, sir," I said and exited his office with some relief. Goodbyes are hard.

On the way to the stairs, I passed Robert Harris' office, the new comptroller. He looked up and smiled, and I smiled back. He'd grown huge "pork chops" since leaving the IRS and taking the position at Stax, but he continued driving his smoking, old Volkswagen Beetle for years. He was a breath of fresh air. We enjoyed a friendship that continues until today.

As I got closer to the parking lot, I picked up speed and hoped I didn't run into the Torpedoes. I felt like I'd been let out early from study hall at school. I was grinning a silly grin when I got to Andrew's car and jumped in. Another half-pint had magically appeared, and I took a gulp.

"Well, how'd it go?" He was excited, too! No more clocking in and clocking out. No more embarrassing searches coming and going, like we were going to steal something.

"Great," I said, "we're free!" And I handed him his final paycheck.

We sat there and looked at each other. We were about to exit Fort Stax (as those of us who had been there the longest had taken to calling the place) for the last time as employees. If we came back, it would be by request only.

Andrew said, "Well, man, I gotta go, so I'll talk to you later!"

I got out of his car and got into mine.

He waved as he pulled up to the electric gate, and Jackson, the security guy, smiled and pushed the button to open it.

I followed but slowed to take a last look at Isaac's gold-plated Eldorado with the wet bar in the narrow back seat. They built a hurricane fence inside the other hurricane fence especially for it. It took four men to lift the hood, and the hubcaps were worth a fortune.

Then I laughed and waved to Jackson to push the button for me and he did, smiling back.

He knew the birds had flown the coop.

I pulled slowly around to the front and looked once more at what I was leaving. I was closing out the first and so important phase of my life. Leaving the nest for the last time. On into the future, and whatever I could make of it.

There was almost no traffic on McLemore. I was in that place where I wasn't really seeing anything that was going by. I was grinning and tingling, and all I could hear was a rushing sound in my ears like I was falling. And why shouldn't I feel like this?

I was twenty-eight-years-old and standing on the edge of the universe.

On The Record With Wayne

My thoughts and comments about some of the songs I worked on and artists I worked with during the Sixties.

TRY A LITTLE TENDERNESS/Otis Redding

The opening line...that's real cloudy to me. I think Isaac Hayes put that together. I'm not sure how the harmonies came about. The counterpoint. But it sounds like something Isaac would have done. It could have just as easily been Otis, because he was a genius. I don't know who decided to do it at that tempo. I do know when Al Jackson changed the drum tempo, nobody was ready for that. It was a mistake. But instead of stopping, we just kept going. And it all worked out great.

That's probably the most famous horn introduction to any song ever. When we did it at the 20th Anniversary of the Monterey Pop Festival with Robert Cray, Robert sang it. And when we started playing the intro, the crowd stood up and cheered. Most of them were at the concert twenty years before with the same camera! Old hippies trying to help each other up to take pictures.

I'VE BEEN LOVING YOU TOO LONG/Otis Redding

We were standing out in the middle of the floor with Otis, and he sang the horn lines to us. Then we added the sustain notes and the modulation notes ourselves. I remember all of us thinking that it was one of his best songs, but it was just another normal day in the studio with Otis...a lot of excitement, because he was such an inflammable singer. He just caught everything on fire when he sang. It is one of my favorite songs of the Stax era. But my all time favorite title is *When Something Is Wrong With My Baby*, by Sam & Dave.

IN THE MIDNIGHT HOUR/Wilson Pickett

This was done at Stax. Wilson came in from New York City. Steve

Cropper and Wilson wrote that song.

I remember my impression of Wilson was that he had a big smile and was always dressed to the nines, looking like he stepped out of a fashion magazine. And I remember him being a bit nervous about being in the South, although he was from Alabama. I think Al Bell told me about that. Wilson really had a thing about the South. I don't know if he thought a farmer was going to rush out of the closet and beat him with a rake or something. That was in him somehow.

KNOCK ON WOOD/Eddie Floyd

That's one of the songs I went to the motel late at night with Steve Cropper and Eddie and played the horn lines along with them. But I think the next day was when somebody came up with that little instrumental that is hard to play in the middle of it. Could have been Isaac, might have been Steve. But we'd worked out the main stuff the night before, so I knew.

Eddie Floyd is the nicest guy of all, of everybody, most sincerely a Southern gentleman, and the kind of guy that when something happened, he would be the first to step up and take a swing. He's a real man. First class. Eddie wouldn't rent a Chevrolet, he'd rent a Cadillac. And he'd have the best looking suit and work the hardest on stage.

LAND OF 1000 DANCES/Wilson Pickett

I thought that was a hit record, cause it had such a high energy groove to it...a great sing along.

It was cut in Muscle Shoals, and there were a whole bunch of us on that record. We cut it all together. And like I said, Wilson was nervous about the South. Muscle Shoals was more South than Memphis, so he probably had his underwear in a snit the whole time. And you know what, it could be that the fear Wilson felt about the South was part of why his records had that edge. Why his screaming was so authentic!

SATISFACTION/Otis Redding

I remember thinking, why in the hell is he covering the Stones on that song when he could write his own. But he was trying for a number one pop record.

SKINNY LEGS AND ALL/Joe Tex

That was cut at American Studio. The first time we met Joe Tex, we cut that record. And it was a big hit. Buddy Killen from Nashville was producing. Don't know how Buddy got a hold of Joe Tex, but he did. They wanted the real thing, the Memphis thing. You couldn't get that in Nashville, especially at that time.

Joe Tex had a big smile, laughed a lot and was a gentleman, a Texas-style gentleman. He was real expansive. He was not a big fellow, taller than me, but not a big guy. But he had a big heart.

Skinny Legs and All was also the record that Reggie Young did a definitive guitar lick on that defined "chicken pickin." That was an original lick. From there after, all licks that went like that were credited to Reggie. That was a seminal moment in recording history.

WALKING THE DOG/Rufus Thomas

I just remember how corny I thought it was. But we had done *The Dog* before that, and it was a hit. Then we did *Walking The Dog*. And that just goes to show you that corn sells.

Rufus was Mr. Clean. He was a disc jockey for a living. Even as his records started hitting, he never did give up disc jockeying. As little boys, Rufus and his buddy, Bones, danced on Beale Street for tips, and Rufus would tell corny jokes, the same ones he told his whole life. Bones was the main hoofer, and they worked that street back when it was in its heyday.

What I learned from him was that show business is fun. And if there's a camera around, get in the frame somehow and look good. Try to look good all the time, because that's what people expect, that you're dressed up in a suit smiling and having a great time. He was king of that. He also could expound on any subject. He was a real diplomat. He was an old time kind of a fellow. He knew how to make people happy. And it wasn't any of this get on the camera and be a civil rights activist, although he certainly was, but he was in a dignified way.

The main thing was to look sharp and be in the camera, as close to the middle as you could get with the loudest clothes. And he had no shame. In other words, Rufus would just do anything to be a clown and get the attention. And that's what an entertainer is all about. He used to wear a hot pink, velvet tuxedo with short pants, and boy when he came on stage, people would go wild. Then he had to back that up by being wild, so he invented the funky chicken. He would get out and do that funky chicken and get people up on the stage to do it with him, and he was a star because of that.

I remember once when Rufus was being interviewed publicly by fellow disc jockey, George Klein, George asked, "Rufus, did Elvis steal the black man's blues?" Rufus waited for the crowd to calm down, and then in a moment of strange seriousness, he pointed his finger to George and said in his growly voice, "Now y'all listen to me, music ain't got no color. It ain't black or white, and it shore ain't blue. Elvis Presley knew how to sing like that when he was born. He was just a natural." Then Rufus went back to being funny.

B-A-B-Y/Carla Thomas

I thought at the time it was a hit, because I just loved Carla and her singing.

FA-FA-FA-FA-FA (SAD SONG)/Otis Redding

Spontaneity at its best. Otis was in the middle of the floor working it out and clapping his hands and just pointing at us saying, "yo turn." We'd play whatever he sang. That was all the forethought that went into that. It was his horn arrangement of *Fa-Fa*. He was a real natural.

HOLD ON I'M COMIN'/Sam & Dave

I thought it was a hit. I thought everything we did with them was a hit except *Soul Man*. I thought that was the dumbest song I ever heard!

SOUL MAN/Sam & Dave

Andrew and I had written a song on that album called *The Good Runs the*

Bad Away. I wanted that to be the single, so I voted for it. Everybody else voted for *Soul Man*, and they were right.

I remember the session, because I was embarrassed by it. *Soul Man* was the current trick phrase. Everybody was calling each other *Soul Man*. "What's happening *Soul Man*?" "How you doin' *Soul Man*?" And I hate that kind of stuff. I was already a full-grown man, and that didn't appeal to me. I thought it was embarrassing...and that's another real lesson that corn sells.

THE HOUSE THAT JACK BUILT/Aretha Franklin

I love that song. I don't know why except that is was fun to do, and it was a fun title. And as a musician, being with Aretha was always great.

On all the Aretha records, we were lucky, very lucky, to have Tom Dowd who was real hip to horns and hip to explaining and conducting horns. And we had Arif Mardin who would sometimes write things out, but he was there to help us. They were New York hip, and we were Southern night club hip. The combination of those two things boiled up a soup that was really great. You put Aretha in the middle of that stew, and you really had something fantastic.

SWEET CAROLINE/Neil Diamond

He was the guy we were impressed with. We did him before Elvis. We were all excited about doing Neil Diamond, as we should have been, because he was the heaviest of the heaviest of all the people we had done at American, really anywhere else at that time. And WE wanted to be heavy. So Neil was a step up for us. He was really nice. He would congratulate us on all the stuff we had done. He was very respectful, and he stayed while we worked, instead of leaving. Even after he did his stuff, he stayed while we did things. He had a good time, so we felt like we had truly interacted with Neil.

I thought *Sweet Caroline* was a hit record. I thought everything we did with him was a hit, because he was Neil Diamond for one thing. And it was a wonderful song. I also liked *Brother Love's Traveling Salvation Show*. I think Mike Leech wrote those horns. I also remember participating in those horn arrangements. It was real interaction with Mike Leech. He was a great arranger of strings and horns. He was a trumpet player in high school, so he had some idea of what it was like to play a horn. So it was fun to play Mike's arrangements. He never tried to overdo anything. He never wrote parts that were too hard, too high or too fast. He wrote something he could play. Just like Andrew and I do. That made it easy on everybody. But they were tasty parts. They were the right things.

THINK/Aretha Franklin

This was done in New York City at Atlantic Records. We did it all together, and then we overdubbed horns, too. We laid down horns, and then went back and overdubbed more horns just to thicken it up. I remember we ganged up around the piano with Aretha. I sat on the bench next to her for awhile, and we all just figured it out. She knew a lot about what she wanted especially from the background singers, her girls. They did their thing, and we put horns together. I think Arif Mardin was there. I know Tom Dowd was. Tom always had a lot of ideas, and of course, Arif is an arranger, period.

Aretha is sweet as she can be, and she's very strong. She's strong at the piano. She plays the piano like a man. She plays with a lot of force...with authority. She knows what she wants. We were on a roll with Aretha, and I knew it was a hit just from the excitement in her voice. It was magic. With Aretha, it always was.

She's real calm in the studio. She knows what she wants and projects enthusiasm and confidence. And of course, she loves to sing more than anything in the world. That's her gift, and there's no one like her. She knows that, too. So she really loves, as a musician, to knock everybody in the studio out. A lot of people are either intimidated by their own skills or intimidated by the musicians. But she's not, because she knows she's the best. She knows that musicians love to hear her sing, so we always felt she was singing for us.

HOOKED ON A FEELING/BJ Thomas

Mark James is a wonderful songwriter. BJ Thomas is a wonderful singer. Chips Moman is a wonderful producer. And the American rhythm section were all ace of spades. So you put all that together, and a song like *Hooked on a Feeling*, and you've got to make a great record.

BJ is one of the nicest guys you ever want to meet. His brother, Jerry, is too. They loved me, and I really don't know why. But we all connected. At an emotional level, we all liked each other.

BJ thought I carried a gun. He thought that was really cool. At that time, everybody was buying guns, and there was a guy on the roof with a gun. After Dr. King was killed, we didn't know when all hell was going to break loose. American Studio was in the ghetto. We didn't know when they might come pouring out of the ghetto ready to kill every white guy they could see, so we were ready to defend ourselves.

One time, years later when I was on tour with Marty Robbins, we were all in the Dallas airport standing around waiting on a plane, and here comes BJ down the hall. He ran up and grabbed me. All the rest of them were in awe of the fact that I even knew BJ Thomas let alone had him hugging on me and asking me, "Are you totin'?" I said, "What?" And he said, "Are you packing? A rod, have you got a rod on you? Are you packing?"

Marty Robbins and the band just couldn't believe it. So we hugged and talked for a few minutes, and then BJ went on to catch his next plane. And I was left standing there looking at Marty and the band trying to figure out what to tell them about that. So I told them a little about the Martin Luther King experience and that somehow BJ had in his mind that I always carried a gun. I guess cause I was a slick dresser at that time.

Of course, I didn't carry a gun. I never carried a gun. I had one in the car. We all did. The riots affected everybody that deeply. Everybody was scared to death for their families and for their personal being.

SON OF A PREACHER MAN/Dusty Springfield

This was done at Sam Phillips Recording Service with Tom Dowd. We had no idea who Dusty Springfield was. We knew that she was some sort of English star. The song was really fun, and Tom was excited about it and about our performance. I don't know how much of that he wrote. I'm sure he took credit for all it, but that's what people did in those days. They took all the credit they could garner, and we didn't know. They were paying us, and we didn't know how important credit was. But we found out. We did Lulu about that time, too. Dusty was never there. I never met her. It was just Tom Dowd with a box under his arm.

WHO'S MAKING LOVE/Johnnie Taylor

It's really hard to say who your favorite blues singer is when there are quite a lot of good ones, but after much tortured thought and hair-pulling, I'm reasonably certain, Johnnie Taylor takes the cake. The first time I heard the line, "Who's making love to your old lady while you were out making love?," I came absolutely unglued! It was during a time when I was certainly guilty of those charges, and it nailed me right between the eyes. So if you think the horn lines are particularly inspired during that session, you're one hundred percent correct!

Johnnie escaped from Crawfordsville, Arkansas, on the wings of his golden voice, good looks and charm. As you'll remember, this is the small town just sixteen miles from my home in West Memphis where my first wife, Linda Christopher, was raised. Johnnie walked across the tops of the cotton bolls on his way out of there heading for stardom.

In my opinion, he must be the best-looking, best-dressed, lady killer, blues singer that God has so far unleashed upon the earth. (I don't mean to slight Little Milton. He's certainly number two!) If you were ever in a room with Johnnie when his eyes lit up and he laughed, you would be transported with him to whatever thought had tickled his fancy. What a laugh!

SUSPICIOUS MINDS & IN THE GHETTO/Elvis Presley

I thought *Suspicious Minds* was a world-class song as opposed to *Teddy Bear* and *Jailhouse Rock*. I thought that was a heavy song, and it spoke to his and Priscilla's situation.

In the Ghetto spoke to our own situation being in the ghetto and what Elvis might have seen had he walked down the street in that neighborhood where we were recording with a guy on the roof holding an automatic weapon. Here we were doing a song about that situation, and I felt he'd sung a song like that. There had never been one come down the pike that those people would have let come into his hands, because it was heavy.

It could have gone the other way. The world could have said, "no we don't like this. This ain't Elvis." But he took the chance. Chips also took a chance. As it turned out, it changed the course of Elvis' life and career. We were sitting there listening to him sing that song, and the electricity was...you could have hung clothes on the electricity that was coming through there. So yeah, we knew it was great.

BORN UNDER A BAD SIGN/Albert King

Albert King is somewhat like me in that if he hadn't discovered a musical instrument, he might have wound up in Arkansas doing something associated with a cotton plant. Instead, he amazed the world with his voice and his winged guitar.

I'll never forget recording *Born Under A Bad Sign* with him at Stax. The song was so perfect, and his voice and guitar were, too. It's something akin to going to church when you're that close to that much power. The power Albert had in his fingers and throat...a religious experience I shall never forget.

Then he drove off across the Mississippi Delta in his old, smokin' humpback bus on his way to thrill fans everywhere he stopped.

He called me his "little whistle tooter," and I was so proud to be that.

He influenced more guitar players than anybody before or since, the original, the one and only, Albert King.

Wayne Jackson Partial Discography

1961 *Last Night*/The Mar-Keys
#2 R&B
Gold Single

Gee Whiz/Carla Thomas
#5 R&B

1963 *Walking the Dog*/ Rufus Thomas
#5 R&B
Gold Single

1965 *I've Been Loving You Too Long*/Otis Redding
#2 R&B

In the Midnight Hour/Wilson Pickett
#1 R&B
#181 RIAA Songs of the Century

Respect/Otis Redding
#4 R&B

Mr. Pitiful/Otis Redding
#10 R&B

Otis Blue/Otis Redding
#1 R&B Album
#74 Rolling Stone Top 500

1966 *When A Man Loves A Woman*/Percy Sledge
#1 Pop & R&B
Gold Single
#51 RIAA Songs of the Century

Land of 1000 Dances/Wilson Pickett
#1 R&B

I'm Your Puppet/James & Bobby Purify
#5 R&B

634-5789/Wilson Pickett
#1 R&B

B-A-B-Y/Carla Thomas
#3 R&B
Gold Single

Hold On I'm Comin'/Sam & Dave
#1 R&B
Gold Single

Mustang Sally/Wilson Pickett
#6 R&B

Knock on Wood/Eddie Floyd
#1 R&B
Gold Single

Fa-Fa-Fa-Fa-Fa/Otis Redding
#12 R&B

Satisfaction/Otis Redding
#4 R&B

Philly Dog/The Mar-Keys
#19 R&B

I Can't Turn You Loose/Otis Redding
#11 R&B

Memphis Soul Stew/King Curtis
#6 R&B

My Lover's Prayer/Otis Redding
#10 R&B

Take Me (Just As I Am)/Solomon Burke
#11 R&B

The Soul Album/Otis Redding
#3 R&B

1967 *Respect*/Aretha Franklin
#1 R&B/Pop
Gold Single
Grammy Winner

Soul Man/Sam & Dave
#1 R&B
Gold Single
Grammy Winner

Try A Little Tenderness/Otis Redding
#4 R&B

Funky Broadway/Wilson Pickett
#1 R&B

The Dark End of the Street/James Carr
#10 R&B

Skinny Legs & All/Joe Tex
#2 R&B
Gold Single

Shake Your Tailfeather/James & Bobby Purify
#15 R&B

Tramp/Otis Redding
#2 R&B

When Something Is Wrong With My Baby/Sam & Dave
#2 R&B

1968 *Dock Of The Bay*/Otis Redding
#1 R&B/Pop
Gold Single
Grammy Winner

Dock Of The Bay/Otis Redding
#1 R&B Album

The History of Otis Redding/Otis Redding
#1 R&B Album

Cry Like A Baby/The Boxtops
#2 Pop

Hooked On A Feeling/BJ Thomas
#5 Pop
Gold Single

I Thank You/Sam & Dave
#4 R&B

The House That Jack Built/Aretha Franklin
#2 R&B

Think/Aretha Franklin
#1 R&B
Gold Single

Men Are Gettin' Scarce/Joe Tex
#7 R&B

See Saw/Aretha Franklin
#9 R&B
Gold Single

Papa's Got A Brand New Bag/Otis Redding
#10 R&B

1969 *Suspicious Minds*/Elvis Presley
#1 Pop
Platinum Single

In The Ghetto/Elvis Presley
#3 Pop
Platinum Single

Sweet Caroline/Neil Diamond
#4 Pop
Gold Single

Holly Holy/Neil Diamond
#6 Pop
Gold Single

Son Of A Preacher Man/Dusty Springfield
#10 Pop

The Weight/Aretha Franklin
#3 R&B

Hot Buttered Soul/Isaac Hayes
#1 R&B

Brother Love's Traveling Salvation Show/Neil Diamond
#22 Pop

Soulful/Dionne Warwick
#2 R&B

Soul Deep/The Boxtops
#18 Pop

1970 *Don't Play That Song*/Aretha Franklin
#1 R&B
Gold Single
Grammy Winner

Cracklin' Rosie/Neil Diamond
#1 Pop

I Just Can't Help Believing/ BJ Thomas
#9 Pop

Kentucky Rain/ Elvis Presley
#3 Adult
Platinum Single

The Letter/ Joe Cocker
#7 Pop

Do The Funky Chicken/ Rufus Thomas
#5 R&B

Cry Me A River/ Joe Cocker
#11 Pop

1971 *Theme From Shaft*/ Isaac Hayes
#1 Pop
Gold Single
Grammy Winner

Shaft/ Isaac Hayes
#1 Pop
#1 R&B
#1 Jazz

Rock Steady/ Aretha Franklin
#2 R&B
Gold Single

Tired Of Being Alone/ Al Green
#7 R&B
Gold Single

Mud Slide Slim/ James Taylor
#2 Pop
Platinum Album

Stephen Stills II/ Stephen Stills
#8 Pop
Gold Album

Live at the Fillmore/ Aretha Franklin & King Curtis
#3 Jazz

1972 *Let's Stay Together*/ Al Green
#1 R&B
Gold Single
Gold Album

I Gotcha'/Joe Tex
#1 R&B
Gold Single

You Ought To Be With Me/Al Green
#1 R&B
Gold Single

I'm Still In Love With You/Al Green
#1 R&B
Gold Single
Gold Album

Look What You've Done For Me/Al Green
#2 R&B
Gold Single

Young, Gifted & Black/Al Green
#2 R&B
Gold Album
Grammy Winner

Blessed Are/Joan Baez
#11 Pop
Gold Album

Black Moses/Isaac Hayes
#1 R&B
Grammy Winner

Rock & Roll Lullaby/BJ Thomas
#1 Adult

1973 *Here I Am*/Al Green
#2 R&B
Gold Single

Call Me/Al Green
#2 R&B
Gold Single
Gold Album

Shotgun Willie/Willie Nelson
#41 Country

Drift Away/Dobie Gray
#5 Pop

I Can't Stand The Rain/Ann Peebles
#6 R&B

1974 *Livin' For You*/Al Green
#1 R&B Album

Eyes Of Silver/The Doobie Brothers
#52 Pop

Let's Get Married/Al Green
#3 R&B

What Were Once Vices Are Now Habits/The Doobie Brothers
#4 Pop
Platinum Album

Smiler/Rod Stewart
#13 Pop

1975 *Atlantic Crossing*/Rod Stewart
#9 Pop
Gold Album

Al Green Explores Your Mind/Al Green
#1 R&B
Gold Album

Al Green Greatest Hits/Al Green
#3 R&B
Gold Album

1976 *Takin' It To The Streets*/The Doobie Brothers
#8 Pop

Firefall/Firefall
#28 Pop
Gold Album

Disco Duck/Rick Dees
#1 Pop
Platinum Album

1977 *Best Of The Doobies*/The Doobie Brothers
#5 Pop
Multi-Platinum Album

Ain't Gonna Bump No More/Joe Tex
#7 R&B
Gold Single

Luna Sea/Firefall
#27 Pop
Gold Album

1984 *City Of New Orleans*/Willie Nelson
#1 Country Single
#1 Country Album
Platinum Album

1986 *So*/Peter Gabriel
#2 Pop
Multi-Platinum Album

Sledgehammer/Peter Gabriel
#1 Pop

Montana Cafe/Hank Williams, Jr.
#1 Country

1987 *Big Time*/Peter Gabriel
#8 Pop

Born To Boogie/Hank Williams, Jr.
#1 Country Single
#1 Country Album
Gold Album

Strong Persuader/Robert Cray
#13 Pop Album
Multi-Platinum Album
Grammy Winner

1988 *Roll With It*/Steve Winwood
#1 Pop Single
#1 Pop Album
Multi-Platinum Album

Angel Of Harlem/U2
#1 Rock

Rattle & Hum/U2
#1 Pop Album
Multi-Platinum Album

Don't Be Afraid Of The Dark/Robert Cray
#33 Pop
Gold Album
Grammy Winner

1989 *Stormfront*/Billy Joel
#1 Pop
Multi-Platinum Album

1990 *Midnight Stroll*/Robert Cray
#32 Pop
Gold Album

1991 *Heartbreak Station*/Cinderella
#19 Pop
Platinum Album

Damn Right I've Got The Blues/Buddy Guy
#2 Heatseekers
Gold Album
Grammy Winner

1992 *The Very Best Of Otis Redding*/Otis Redding
Platinum Album

1993 *Blues Summit*/BB King
#64 R&B
Multi-Platinum Album
Grammy Winner

1994 *Longing In Their Hearts*/Bonnie Raitt
#1 Pop
Multi-Platinum Album
Grammy Winner

Funny How Time Slips Away/Al Green & Lyle Lovett
Grammy Winner

Rhythm Country & Blues/Various Duets
#1 Country

Give Up But Don't Give Out/Primal Scream
#22 Heatseekers
Gold Album

1995 *Still Got The Blues*/Gary Moore
#83 Pop
Gold Album

1996 *Mercury Falling*/Sting
#5 Pop
Platinum Album

1997 *Disciplined Breakdown*/Collective Soul
#16 Pop
Platinum Album

Sweet Potato Pie/Robert Cray
#3 Blues Album

1999 *Take Your Shoes Off*/Robert Cray
#2 Blues Album
Grammy Winner

2000 *Sailing To Philadelphia*/Mark Knopfler
#60 Billboard

2001 *Presumed Innocent*/Marcia Ball
#4 Blues Album
Handy Winner

2005 *Prairie Wind*/Neil Young
#11 Billboard
Juno Award Winner
Grammy Nominee

2008 *Consolers Of The Lonely*/The Raconteurs
#7 Billboard
Grammy Nominee

2009 *Soulbook*/Rod Stewart
#4 Billboard

2010 *Living Proof*/Buddy Guy
Blues Album Of The Year

32533530R00112

Made in the USA
Lexington, KY
24 May 2014